THE HOJOKI
RE-MEMBERED

THE HOJOKI
RE-MEMBERED

GILLIAN BARLOW

SADDLE ROAD PRESS

Saddle Road Press
Ithaca, New York
saddleroadpress.com

Author photograph by Jamie Clifford
jamiecliffordphoto.com

Cover photograph by Gillian Barlow

Book design by Don Mitchell

ISBN 978-1-7365258-6-9

Library of Congress Control Number: 2022940612

CONTENTS

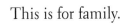

This is for family.

INTRODUCTION

home | hole | hale | hall | hell | sell |self
home | hole | hale | hall | hell | heal | seal | sell | self

All paths lead to "self."

I want to write about how to get from one place to another—changing step by step as I go from "home" to "self." Fingers crossed I will arrive there, at the "somewhere" I want to be, a home of sorts, my self.

I want to do this slowly since that has been the process and not always have I arrived where I want to be.

Ceci n'est pas une carte.

This is not a map. This is a translation.

TRANSLATING

TRANSLATION (I)

I WANT TO APPROACH TRANSLATION in a different way to the usual. As the world becomes more diverse and accepting of this diversity, translation becomes more important. It is no longer enough to anticipate someone will speak the same language as you. You are expected to know more than one language and if you don't know anything except your one language, you need to sort out other ways of communicating with people.

There was a time when the closest most of us came to translation was in subtitled films. Many people refused to attend them. They go to a film to relax and having to read as well as watch a film isn't what they want to pay for. I find films in a foreign language exciting. There is a split in the brain that occurs when you are watching the film as well as reading the subtitles at the bottom. I find this better than watching a dubbed film where although you are not required to read, you get caught up in watching how closely someone's mouth follows the words of a different language and when it comes down to it, they don't follow very closely for very long at all.

There are books written about the process of translating a document from one language into another. I cannot even pretend to do this with the small amount of non-English languages I speak although I like the idea of fluently speaking another tongue.

I think of appropriated writing as a form of translation. Appropriated writing is a tradition of taking fragments of writing from here and there and putting them together to form something else. In a literary translation, it is expected you will match exactly what someone else has written—or at the very least their intent. It is expected the translator will be invisible. The sum is to be exactly the same as the parts. This is of course impossible. There is much written about the process and product of translation. I have heard it said it was the translations not the originals that made Marquez's writing so famous. Both writer and translator would probably find this horrifying.

I am using translating differently to this. I am using it as I see it occur in my life in the following ways:

The translation of one language into another.

The translation of a text written in Japanese into one written in English.

The translation of a written score into sound.

The translation of words into a book.

The translation of a book into film.

The translation of two-dimensional ideas and thoughts into a three-dimensional model and then a full-scale example, the building, as done by an architect.

The translation of Japanese kanji and hiragana into photos of Aboriginal housing.

The translation of an exegesis from academic language into a language more accessible by everyday people.

The translation of a Japanese text into poetry.

The translation of houses into homes.

The translation of myself into the being I want to be.

I find translation an interesting process. It uses intuition and knowledge at the same time. It opens you to thinking in a different way. Each time I do the translation part, I find it exciting. Once you start thinking about translation, everything can be considered one—the translation of a recipe into the edible meal: the translation of thoughts into words: the translation of a plan into reality....

TRANSLATION (II)

A TIBETAN WOMAN is speaking. She has her back to us who are sitting on the ground around her. She is facing a woman who sits at the front of the room. The Tibetan woman wears her traditional dress especially for the occasion—a long black pleated dress with an apron of red, yellow, gold, blue, further decorated with embroidery. She wears a turquoise necklace. She has metallic bangles from wrist to elbow on both of her arms. Her black hair is pulled back tightly against her head and held there with an array of beaded clasps. She holds her hands in front of her. Sometimes her fingers interlock. Sometimes her right hand, and then her left, describes arcs and curves in the air. Sometimes both hands hang loosely, defeated, at her sides. Sometimes, and this most often, her hands are pressed together in prayer, fingertip matching fingertip, palm of hand to palm of hand, making a heart shape at her chest.

She starts to speak, stops then starts again. This time she talks more confidently, speaking in Tibetan while the woman sitting in a high-backed chair at the front, nods and listens to the Tibetan. She too speaks this language and understands what the Tibetan woman says. Although we understand none of these Tibetan words, the conversation brings tears to our eyes. She speaks as much with her hands as with her voice, mouth, tongue, teeth, lips, heart. She begins to cry. We also start crying. She continues speaking as we cry.

The woman in the highbacked chair facing towards us begins to translate:

"She says, she is saying, here in this country, in this place, she has nowhere to practice as she does at home —at the place she comes from. Everyone at home would be practicing all the time and she can't anymore. This makes her sad. She would like to go home but she can't. They won't let her. Her family is here. There is no way back. She is here with us now. She is trying to make a place, her home, here with us. She is saying, that here, today, in this place, at this moment, she is feeling like she can be happy. She feels almost as though she were at home, here, with us—not entirely, this place will never be home but today here with you, us, in this moment, her body feels as though it has settled. It is almost "home."

Or that is what I remember as what was said. Her body showing her to be both upset and thankful.

She could have easily been saying she wanted to leave here and go back to Tibet.

The Hojoki

I HAVE KNOWN ABOUT the Hojoki, the Ten Foot Square Hut, since I went to architecture school and my tutor spoke about it. I found a copy when I finished my architectural studies and was overseas in London. It is 21 pages long, written by a Buddhist monk living in the hills above Kyoto, Japan during the thirteenth century. Chomei, the author, comments on the fickleness of the world. He had started life living in luxury and through misfortune or bad planning now finds himself living alone in a small hut of ten foot by ten foot yet he finds himself totally content.

We were told about it in architecture school because our first project in final year was to design ourselves the smallest possible dwelling we could imagine. It was so we could explore fundamental questions such as: What did we really need for life? Did we need all the amenities we were told by society we had to have? As we did this project, we stayed at the tutor's remote house on the edge of Sydney and lived fully immersed in a minimal lifestyle.

What I learnt from the Hojoki:

Simple is not easy.

Simple can take a long time to get to—usually much longer than a more complicated solution.

Consistency is hard.

There is a place for everything.
Everything in its place.
Small is beautiful.

My smallest possible dwelling was symmetrical around a common kitchen, dining and living room—a sleeping area on one side; bathroom on the other. I had a chance to build and then stay in something similar a few years later. I learnt some minimal building skills doing this. Beautiful timbers were sourced from a local timber mill. Everything was done by hand on the site. Water was sourced from down the hill at a small creek. This is where we also washed at the end of the day. Everything needed to be done consciously—just as Chomei writes. Everything needed a place. Everything needed to be returned to that place.

I stayed there with friends as we built it. It was a labour of love—a sign of the times. We were young.

We grew up and moved back into a world of things. The house my partner and I bought together decades later is also small but neither consistent nor ordered.

As I worked on housing projects within Aboriginal communities throughout Australia, I tried where possible to apply these lessons. Most people in Australia do not value "small." The idea of small being beautiful (Schumacher, 1993) was there as I worked on health buildings where everyone, particularly doctors and specialists, wanted a visual display of their individual importance. Each said they absolutely needed more and more space. "Space" represented "power" and the more space you had, the bigger your office or house, the more important you were.

I continue to be attracted to small simple houses rather than the ever-increasing-in-size complicated ones we are led to believe are best. I see a small beach house of a single room more attractive than the many roomed ones with every modern convenience.

Given how much travel I did through my working life, the type of work I was doing, what I learned about myself, and how I felt about things, it was obvious that my Ph.D. would be about this.

I was required to do 70,000 words of fiction and a 30,000 words exegesis. I managed to write the fiction quickly enough but struggled considerably with the exegesis. I would sit to write each day and could clock up 1,500 words only to delete them all the following day. The process seemed interminable. I was bored writing it so of course the writing was boring. I would never finish it. To be fair to myself, I was working full time while I did my PhD and had only snatches of time to spend on it when I got home from work or over the weekend. After what seemed to be eons, I decided to devote myself full time for a limited period to its completion. I felt if I took on the exegesis as a full-time job, I might be able to slog at it and just "do it."

It didn't work. Day in, day out, I continued to delete what I had done the previous day before I could write. The writing continued to be boring—so tedious, a struggle.

And then one day sitting in a lecture, an interesting one by an overseas guest, everything dropped into place. I had an idea. It suddenly seemed this exegesis writing could be exciting. I abruptly left the lecture and ran home to check whether what I thought I could do might be possible. I sat with the idea for a few days, afraid if I were to tell my supervisor what I was thinking, she would shake her head and quell my enthusiasm.

I finally plucked up enough courage to ring her and she agreed what I wanted to do was worth a try—I would "translate" the Japanese text version I had found of the Hojoki into photos of Aboriginal housing and write about my process for doing this.

Translation (A Start!)

When I began, I thought the text I was looking at was in ideograms.

An ideogram, rather than a group of letters arranged according to phonemes of a spoken language, as in alphabetic languages such as English, is a graphical symbol representing an idea.

An ideogram might have a picture or words and the meaning is understood through common knowledge. Arabic numbers are ideograms because their meaning is known even though there are so many different languages in which to say them. We all know "1." It is *one* or *eins* or *un* or *uno* or…. The numeral, 1, says the same thing to us in all our different languages.

When I started my translating, I was captivated by ideograms. While I soon came to understand what I was looking at were not ideograms, I found I continued to think of them as such. Still, as I was not doing a translation as it is usually done and was therefore not constrained by any understanding of what each might mean, I could make of them what I chose. I made up a narrative for each as I examined them closely. I looked for the small bowls of rice sitting in front of a human, the bird's eye view of a rice field, an ideogram for describing movement, the moon, all of which a German architect, Nitschke (1966) wrote of in his article on *Ma* (a Japanese sense of place). I wondered why each ideogram was as it was. I wondered about each's history. Why had moon become sun, for example, as it peeped between the two gate posts in the word for *ma*?

As I continued to translate, I learned more about what I was doing. The Japanese written language is not made up of one system but many—a multiplicity. There is hiragana, kanji and katakana. Each of these has its own history. In general, in Japan small children begin learning to write by using hiragana. There are 46 basic hiragana. Katakana is mostly used for foreign words co-opted into Japanese. Hiragana and katakana could be looked at as "alphabetic" systems.

Kanji are largely based on the Chinese characters. There are approximately 2,500 Japanese kanji and high school children in Japan will be expected to know 1,945 of them. Kanji can be pronounced in two ways—either as *onyomi* or *kunyomi*. *Onyomi* is the Chinese reading of a kanji. *Kunyomi* is the Japanese reading of them. If I were a Chinese person, I might be able to read each kanji but I will not necessarily be understood by a Japanese person since my pronunciation of it may be totally different. What I know as "ma" may sound like a *kan/ken* (*onyomi*) or *ma* (*kunyomi*). Sometimes a single text can be written in a mixture of the different scripts.

Japanese kanji are dense symbols and have evolved over time. I did not know what any of the words I knew in Japanese might look like. In hindsight this was probably an advantage as I wasn't hindered by attempting to be accurate.

Once I started on my ideogram translation, I didn't stop writing for three weeks until I had finished it. The work included the translation, substituting into the

Japanese text tiny photos of Aboriginal housing and other things I had seen on my visits into remote and very remote places of Australia. In the process I referred to other photos, paintings and texts—it was after all an academic text so it was expected there would be references to theories and information other than myself. It had become what I wanted it to be—a multi-disciplinary piece: one that might weave throughout the many different strands of interest I have without needing to fit into a formal suit.

I never anticipated I would be able to speak Japanese from doing any of these translations. However, I did hope in the future I might be able to look at a piece of Japanese text and gain some innate sense of what it was trying to convey. I cannot even claim my translating of the text has revealed anything significant to me, although I cannot be certain about this. It has made me conscious of how difficult a language Japanese is—knowing words, even knowing some of the grammar, doesn't make you know a language.

I did love the experience of this writing. It was almost magical, as though someone was guiding me. I was taken over by something outside of myself and wrote larger than me. It was fantastic. Any time I talk about this original "translation" even now some years later, I feel my excitement mounting.

I was given the opportunity to publish it but to do so I needed to do considerable work on it. For example, I needed to edit it out of its academic suit. I also had to rid it of all the paintings and photos because of copyright issues and to make sure it was readable by a broader audience —the list went on. I was keen but again, because I was working full time, it was a substantial period before I got very far.

I began to see I had now embarked on another translation.

Translation (Revision)

THE NEXT TRANSLATION was not one of the Hojoki but a translation of my academic exegesis from academic language into more accessible language. This sounds easy but proved more difficult than I imagined. Although I believed the original to be non-academic it quickly became obvious it was still extremely academic not in only words but also in the way it was constructed. There were the issues of copyright to consider. There were many photos within the original and while these needed no copyright if used in an academic text, there are lengthy and costly copyright issues if published within the public domain. It meant I had to go through and question each photo or painting and decide whether it was essential to what I was trying to do.

I felt trepidation. I felt it would be better to forget the translation aspect and focus on the memoir/fictional material buried within. Maybe translation could return as a loose joining factor later if necessary.

I was wrong. As quickly as I dropped out all mention of translation, it returned, insisting to be included in my work as an architect.

What? This isn't how people usually think of an architect.

Let me explain. As an architect I am required to translate your words into a two-dimensional representation, the plan, which I have been trained to understand in the third dimension. This part is as important as the first because although many people can understand a plan and know what it is they want, they are not always good at envisioning it into the third dimension. An architect, in theory, adds value in knowing this. It takes time and experience to do. Architecture is not simple.

Then for me to work in an Aboriginal community, or any non-English speaking community, a separate translator is needed to get the words of the client into English so I as an English-speaking person can translate them into two and then three dimensions.

I am not sure I was always successful in explaining what the house or building I was doing might be like, to those who were going to live there, when I returned to the Community. First, I needed to translate into words what I was trying to do in my two-dimensional plan. Then my English words had to be translated into a language the client could understand. I never felt as though I had enough tools to do this well. For many of the houses I designed, I would produce a small cardboard model to show more clearly the house's three-dimensional form and to help people understand how their plan might work; what it might feel like to be inside and how they would go about their daily life there—what they might expect to see. Sometimes I would make a rough outline on the ground, and we would "walk-through" the house—me talking about what we were doing—here we look to the left and see the kitchen door....

A lot of trust must be given to an architect for this to work. It takes time—and of course, time is money. Not all projects had sufficient budget to be able to do this properly.

When I finished my book or what I thought of as finished I sent it off to the publisher. It wasn't well received. I was disappointed but it was true. The manuscript was disjointed with no clear intent—something I had learnt as an architect to do but had failed to consider even vaguely in my writing.

Writing is different to architecture of course. In architecture, considerable time is spent up front on design. The process is then a slow one of converting the idea into sketches, developing the details which are the makings of the building into drawings readable by a builder to construct into the finished building. There should be a consistency in these just as in writing. Writing, however, is a process of continuously writing, writing over, expansion and reduction and then re-writing—a slow translation of thoughts into words and then more, and different, words to polish up and make the thoughts clear.

I hadn't realized the extent of drafting and re-drafting, revising and then re-revising that would be needed. I embarked on the second re-writing without re-visioning what it was I was writing, without being clear on what it was I was doing. I slogged at this for two subsequent drafts. Each one was completed but each failed to move the process very far. Although the writing itself became clearer, the whole book was not.

We are not used to the idea that things—a building, a book, an artwork—take considerable time—genius or not. It becomes quicker perhaps as we get older because we are more experienced at it. We have done it before. But it still takes time.

I always argue for this as an architect. I failed to appreciate it was also true for writing.

Translation (Poems)

I WORKED AT THE NEXT TRANSLATION for a considerable time in much the same way as I had the original writing of my exegesis.

Again, I began to feel like Sisyphus. This task did give me an excuse to stay at home and hide from the world, suiting my introverted self. However, after years it began to feel like a joke. It would never be finished and surely there were other things in life to devote myself to. My drafts would get close to being finished and then suddenly veer away. What was it I was not saying so I could never actually finish?

As before at a point of total despair, I had a new idea for translation. I had been avoiding anything to do with my original translation of the Hojoki because of the many issues it held. These seemed impossible to surmount. If I couldn't say what was needed to be said, then perhaps I could have the Hojoki say it instead.

This current translation, the one I see as the third translation, started much the same as the original translation, where I inserted not only my experiences but other people's, in the form of paintings and photographs, into the text. This time I played with a myriad of ways to substitute something in for the kanji to circumnavigate the copyright issues. I spent days changing kanji into a solid shape in Adobe. As the text became a more complex file it took longer and longer to save; longer and longer to exchange a colored shape for an individual kanji.

I thought it might help things if I did this substitution manually. I bought small stamps to cover over the kanji. I tried texts. I tried stickers—all in desperation to replicate the original translation. I wondered what I was trying to add by doing this. It would circumnavigate copyright laws but added little more. The original using photos and paintings gave a richness to the translation—the new substitutions paled in comparison.

Perhaps…perhaps…a different type of translation. I would abandon the shapes/paintings/colors type of substitution and have the text talk directly to me instead.

Using the same kanji I used in the original translation, I located them in the Japanese text I had and correlated them with a line in the English translation of the text by A. L. Sadler (1979) I had. For example, if a kanji appeared in line two of the Japanese text, I cross referenced it with line 2 in the English text and selected words in the second line. Having been through the entire Japanese text, and then the corresponding English text, I used these words, and only these words, to write a poem. More rules developed over time as I did this—the rules changed from kanji to kanji.

I found as I continued translating in this way that many of the kanji were in the same lines of the English text and the poems began to seem too similar. It was true I was hoping to find some resonance, an alignment, between the Japanese text and its English translation and my understanding of them, but I didn't want all the poems to be the same.

It is strange how familiar the words of the poems sound, particularly in these unprecedented times of coronavirus.

It is as though the Japanese Hojoki is me speaking whilst in lockdown where I watch from within my own ten-foot square writing room through a skylight to the sky outside. Life is bleak. Yet there is always hope. Problems seemingly so important fade into a single point: surviving without illness. We have had no precedence to prepare us for this pandemic. We are all human. So much worry about the economy when it is really our health and how we look after ourselves and each other we should be concerned with. If we are not alive then there is no economy. Politicians fail to see this.

I am writing therefore through a thirteenth century text into the twenty first century, with advice from a monk to myself. Our visions of our individual worlds feel similar. Like Chomei, I have a preoccupation with houses and what they mean about us and our times. A house displays our preoccupations. I have been involved with doing houses for most of my architectural life. While Chomei's circumstances changed significantly when he arrived in his ten-foot square hut with little else except himself to define him, I have built a carapace of books and objects around me and know little about myself, like a cicada shedding my nymph skin regularly but staying much the same inside.

Ceaselessly the river flows, and yet the water is never the same, while in the still pools the shifting foam gathers and is gone, never staying for a moment. Even so is man and his habitation. (The Hojoki, 1)

TRANSLATION

TRANSLATING *No*

の

I hear the cuckoo
his note reminds me
of the everchanging scenery of the hills
the mind knows fatigue

This character, の, is a hiragana—English text *no*; translation—"of."

Each time *no* occurred, I highlighted it. Once I had been through the Japanese text and had identified every *no*, I numbered the lines, noted where *no* occurred and counted through the Japanese text as though it were a haiku. I produced a table of the rolling haiku and identified when *no* was in the fifth, seventh, twelfth lines. If the *no* character was in the fifth line, I counted through the English text and selected words from the fifth line in the English translation. When I had been through the English in the same patterned haiku rhythm and had all the lines, I wrote a poem from the words gathered.

Only when I had finished poetry writing, did I go back to look at the meaning of *no*.

But in working backwards, how was I to know this represented such a common short word—the preposition "of." It seemed so promising when I picked it out. It turned out it was not even what I took it for—it was not a kanji, it was not an ideogram—I had barely begun my translation and everything was already wrong.

No is a hiragana.

When I look at *no*, it reminds me of a mung bean sprout, genus Phaseolus, *Vigna radiata*. Mung bean sprouts are small, mainly white with a delicate green tail. They can be used in savory or sweet meals. Mung beans are full of potential—just like any other sprout, they are a good source of nutrition. Sprouts were used by Captain Cook and any number of seafaring crews to fight off scurvy as they roamed at sea.

"Mung bean sprouts are good for you," said in a motherly voice every child knows and hates.

Mung beans are not necessarily everyone's cup of tea, being weirdly crunchy and a little like eating grass.

My mung bean character nuzzles up to the other characters in the text and adds value to them.

If you isolate this hiragana and see it on its own as I was doing, it looks cute and friendly like a family member. It giggles. Some people warn that mung bean sprouts should be avoided as they can cause illness from salmonella or other bacteria unless they are very fresh and you are certain you know where they have been growing. If grown in sewerage or something similar, they can become poisonous—soaking up the toxins they are living in. Knowing it has the potential to kill makes this hiragana sinister and therefore more interesting. The straight-line curls up (snap) into its mouth—the curve gently reminding us it can lash out at any time. It is keeping quiet here, its mouth held shut—but give it a chance and it will say what it really thinks and it won't be pretty.

Once the mung bean uncurls and develops into a fully-fledged mung bean plant, it can be eaten in salads or cooked into a range of delicious and nutritious meals. Fully grown mung beans can be made into desserts or better can become glass noodles—but we are jumping ahead—here we have only the small mung bean sprout, still with all of this ahead of it. Still brimming with potential.

GARDENING

MY GARDEN HOLDS A LOT OF POTENTIAL. Here I have a chance to achieve something and prove I can be successful. Everything is readily available. There is general soil mix to use. There are pots provided by the woman next door. There are some frail tools that might last for a few digs. I have time. I dream about the things I can grow.

In my first attempts I fail to research up front and plant things needing shade in the sunny spots, those needing sun in the shady ones. I don't think about what colors go with which and know nothing about companion plants. Mostly everything fails. Even things guaranteed to grow, do so by running amok or fail to take off.

I don't give up. I am certain I can do this. I don't have much knowhow but there have been others before me who have done this—who have started from nowhere and been successful in growing flowers and plants to eat. I read Jamaica Kincaid and see her successes; see how her usual obsessiveness assists.

I plant my seeds in a large blue glazed pot. OK—so they are very much closer to each other than the packet suggests but I figure not all of them will germinate and any which do, I will be able to thin by carefully putting them into another pot. The packets say it will take at least nine weeks before I will have a crop.

I don't know exactly what to expect. I forget what is planted where. I know I planted carrots and something called micro greens. I don't know how I will be able to distinguish between them. It shouldn't matter too much, I decide, as if anything sprouts at all I will be happy.

But when some do, I am not.

The seeds take longer to germinate than I expect. Finally, when there are small little bits of green, I feel so very proud I have achieved this. Each one blinking *Sucess*! I can already see the salad I will make with what I have grown. But then it seems to take a lot longer than the nine weeks mentioned on the back of the packet to get anywhere further. Finally, I recognize carrot tops. Their leaves looking like carrot leaves. The mix of micro greens are more difficult to recognize. The seeds as seedlings are in clusters together and will be impossible to separate since their tiny leaves are too entangled. Having put so much effort into getting them to this stage I don't want to lose any of them. I sit in the morning sun worrying about how I can move some of them out of the big mass into small pots and how they will feel alone. I read some vegans believe broccoli has a central nervous system and therefore broccoli can no longer be eaten on a vegan diet. I feel this exactly about my seedlings. I haven't been successful with the few radishes I try to germinate.

I find the one radish I thought was going strongly is actually a dandelion.

WRITING

PLANTS AND MUNG BEAN SPROUTS express the cycle of life in a never-ending loop and nothing different is anticipated of them. They have unknown beginnings and ends. They have potential and their potential is tightly charted.

Writing also tends to be tightly charted. If you are a writer of potential, you will be expected to write in a particular way. In the Mills and Boon storyline, the nurse is always a woman—the doctor always a man. Despite a few awkward moments and misunderstandings, things always iron themselves out. The pair fall deeply in love and marry, have kids and live happily ever after. There is the expected narrative arc—the one where most of the book is spent getting to its crest, a small part with the wave crashing and finally lapping at the beach's edge— serene, calm, concluded. No loose ends!

Is this what we want? For everything to be in this wave? And if we seek then we must find everything resolved?

The Mills and Boon Doctor/Nurse romance book is not everything!

There are other ways of writing. Writing doesn't always have to resolve itself. There is writing differently. Writing from other potentiality.

ZUIHITSU

Zuihitsu is one example of such non-arc driven writing. Zuihitsu comes from the Japanese. The Hojoki, the ten-foot square hut, is considered to be a zuihitsu, as is Sei Shonigan's *The Pillow Book*, which is considered to be the first example of a zuihitsu.

Zuihitsu has definitions but the definitions reveal little. Most appear to say you can do just as you want. *The Pillow Book* has lists and memoir and fragments. Lists are one aspect of a zuihitsu every definition seems to agree on.

Chomei's *The Hojoki* has no lists.

Zuihitsu, like life, does not proceed along the tidy narrative line that many insist it should. We wallpaper over the parts of our lives that don't fit in tidily, those stains and damp patches on the walls. When someone asks, we say we have the wallpaper there because we like the pattern, the color is good, it is so much faster to wallpaper than trying to paint the walls, but in reality, it is because the stains, the damp were getting to be embarrassing.

In doing this, we start to have secrets, we start to tell lies.

For example, life is fragmented, though through writing and storytelling we are at pains to make it appear a smooth continuous surface.

Fragments of text, remnants of memory, bones of a story. The use of the fragment asks you to remember from word to word, and the accumulation of images and stories allows you to construct and formulate, to become

GILLIAN BARLOW

a detective, passing for a moment into some imagined
subjectivity where your personal safety is jeopardised.
At heart you are still the reader of the text and able to
remember who you once were; it isn't a very big jump to
make. You are always fragmented. A sense of solidity is
disrupted when you look away and remember an event
which happened years before. Fragmentation occurs
with memory and memory produces its own fragments
of story that need re-framing for consumption (Prosser,
2009).

FICTOCRITICISM

Fictocriticism is another example of writing without
resolution.

Fictocriticism aligns with how things occur in my
life.

Fictocriticism is a riddle.

Fictocriticism is a way of writing for which there
is no blueprint. It must be constantly invented
anew in the face of the singular problems that
arise in the course of engagement with what is
researched. It is writing as research, stubbornly
insisting on the necessity of a certain process
in these days when writing is treated by those
who determine what counts as research to be a
transparent medium, always somehow after the
event, a simple "outcome" of a research which
always takes place elsewhere, in the archive, in
the field or the focus group, on the web (Gibbs,
2005).

The history of fictocritical writing, like most everything
about fictocriticism, is blurry. While information is

scant, it does have a lineage. Significant writers have used
it. Fictocriticism was there in early Japanese zuihitsu
texts such as *The Pillow Book*. Fictocriticism lurks in the
silence of suppressed women's writing. It burst onto the
Australian scene with *Frictions*, the anthology of women's
writing edited by Gibbs (1982). It has been around ever
since and yet, it is always new:

And it began to make its way into the universities,
initially through women's studies courses, and then
through the advent of courses in creative writing.
Most recently it has manifested in philosophy, history,
anthropology, as a topic in special issues of journals like
Westerly and at conferences, and most significantly in
the so-called "autobiographical turn" of cultural studies
(Gibbs, 1997).

In a fictocritical piece, I can do anything I want to do.
I can experiment, play and theorize, tell anecdotes and
memories and have the fragments considered a complete
text—just as a patchwork quilt with its myriad patches is
considered complete. I can be in one place and move
to another without having to apologize. It is not always
fun and games. It is meant to walk a fine line, an edge,
between theorizing and playing. It is both and neither.

Fictocriticism is the "and/as well" rather than the "and/
or" of theoretical writing. It is never simply one way. There
is always the other side of the coin, and whilst we may
not always believe in it entirely, the other side of the coin
does need to be acknowledged, discussed and included.
It is the full swing, both ways of the pendulum—if the
pendulum motion is the best you can come up with.

Fictocriticism might most usefully be defined as
hybridised writing that moves between the poles
of fiction (invention/speculation) and criticism

(deduction/ explication), of subjectivity (interiority) and objectivity (exteriority). It is writing that brings the creative and the critical together—not simply in the sense of placing them side by side, but in the sense of mutating both, of bringing a spotlight to bear upon the known forms in order to make them say something else (Kerr & Nettelbeck, 1998, 3-4).

It is clear to me that this is how I write but I find it hard to explain to others why I write in such a way. To be truthful, I see no other way for me.

To be truthful, fictocriticism reflects exactly how things are to me and to write in any other way means I would have to twist things around to suit others' experience of how things are.

But now I haven't arrived at where I wanted to be, which was "appropriate." I wanted to talk about appropriate because it is an expectation for writing.

Only certain writing is considered appropriate.

But what is appropriate? How is it different from appropriated?

APPROPRIATED WRITING

適切な — *Tekisetsuna*. This is "appropriate" but I never managed to find such a combination in the Hojoki text.

I do go on to find something more specific with my mung bean.

特定の — *Tokutei no*

Here my mung bean of potential cosies up with some other kanji to say, "I know what you need—I'm certain!" But no matter how hard I try, I never can get from being "certain" to being "appropriate."

No is not appropriate.

Why did I want it to be appropriate?

Why do I want to be appropriate?

Appropriate, from the Latin *appropriare*: to make something fit, to make something one's own.

Or before that, even: *proprius*: to belong to a person, thing, or group.

All my life I believed I wanted to belong, to be proprius. No matter what group, I never belonged. Not the Buddhist group. Not the aikido group. Not the architecture group. Not the orchestra. Not the staff luncheon group. I never fit, was never appropriate. Or I excluded myself before there was ever a chance. I would exclude myself right from the beginning.

Perhaps it is the reason I enjoy appropriated writing.

Academic writing can be considered a type of appropriated writing, as it takes as a springboard known and often hallowed texts, and uses them to dive somewhere new.

Translation can be seen as a type of appropriated writing. In translation, however, the text is rarely reshaped. The shapes the words make are already laid out in a set pattern—the thoughts already thought.

There are so many different appropriated writings.

I enjoy the cut and paste mix of others' writing in erasure poems or computer-generated combinations of pieces. This writing rides on the edge of falling into misappropriation. I am always one for those edges!

I worry that this has to more do with my life and how I understand my life than I admit. I worry that I am appropriating someone else's life but I don't know how to escape it.

...All the difficulties of life spring from this fleeting evanescent nature of man and his habitation. (The Hojoki, 11.)

Translating *Ma* and *Uma*

間

With ashes against this black background
the fire with immense violence raged
and of the houses within its reach
there were none

Pleasure grounds were turned into rice fields
Hear the joyous clamour
Keep off the sun
The forest trees reach close up
Bewailing the vanity of this fleeting life

I have neither fear nor resentment
My only luxury is sound sleep
What shall I have to regret?
This thatched hut is some type of sin

This character, 間, is a kanji—English text *ma*;
translation—"a sense of place."

馬

A most extraordinary thing
While babies continued to feed
The hills crumbled
Pheasants were mistaken for fathers

And in this impermanent hut of mine
Looking like a mendicant priest
I abandoned the world and retired

This character, 馬, is a kanji—English text *uma*; translation "horse."

There is no direct translation of the first of these kanji — 間, *ma*. Many architects have grappled with it.

It's a tricky one for me, though, since it is pronounced "ma" and my partner's name is Ma—and for him it means horse. But he is Chinese and the *Ma* I know or thought I knew is Japanese.

There are two of them therefore, both the same and completely different:

間 and 馬

My name is Ma.

(*Ma* as horse is *uma* in Japanese)

The first *ma* is made up of two parts. The strokes of the first part don't quite mirror each other. I am stopped by this not-quite mirroring.

One is the same as the other except....

They are a gateway or doorway to walk through but the gateway is blocked.

Originally the two mirrored images were part of a character which implied "entrance"—but over time, the two together came to mean the great gate of a Buddhist temple precinct. They have aged and, as they aged, they have moved on from their humble beginnings. They are grand now. They are ceremonial.

Yet, in this *ma*, this great gate, the one stroke on the right-hand side of the gate is ever so slightly deformed.

The right-hand post has a small tail, a gammy foot. I wonder how it does not fall over. The one on the left stands straight and proud as a ceremonial gate post ought. It has been set into hard ground to some depth and will never fall, even if horse riders run into it or swordsmen take swipes at it as they gallop through. The other, the one on the right-hand side, is balancing precariously.

It may be only that the calligrapher who wrote this version of Hojoki with a *ma* like this, placed this ever so small return there on the right, as if to say, "this is my *ma*," a pissing at the doorstop, so it is clear who has made the text.

Or maybe the calligrapher has put the slight deformity there to signify the symbol's humble beginnings, so it won't forget from whence it came.

But when I look through other pieces of the text, I cannot find this small tail.

Perhaps it is a typo.

Perhaps it is not a gammy foot but a helping hand. Perhaps it is there to help the other side of the undercroft, the other character, push its way between the two ceremonial gateposts in the middle of the *ma*, as this central part of the character also has a deformity, a leg that is ever so slightly shorter on one side than the other. Perhaps it is a hand to help prop up the small character.

The two small rectangles in this central piece of the letter are said to be a symbol for the moon. Why square? I wonder. The moon rarely looks square even if seen through an entrance. Why divided into two? I wonder.

Then we are told by Nitschke (1966) in his article on *ma*, as if in response to our unspoken question: "not, as it is sometimes thought, for sun as it is now written." There is no more explanation than this.

I know these two, 馬 and 間, and I know them as having the same sound although even this could be wrong; my insensitive ear may be unable to hear the different intonations as they are spoken. One sound is Cantonese, one is Japanese.

I hear them as the same word, therefore for me they are the same. How often does this happen in colonization? How often does the colonizer not hear properly what is said and assumes the answer? How often does the colonizer not appreciate that what they are hearing from the about-to-be-colonized is not the answer to their question but a wondering repetition of the words they have just said? Not "my name is X" as they have expected, but "what is your name?" repeated back to them.

"What is your name" said with the words like stones in the mouth, strange bulbous rocks rolling around in the mouth, filling it so it is almost impossible to open the mouth without the rocks falling out. The words like a hole in a tooth your tongue keeps going to, reminding you over and over that it is there, your tongue feeling the hole over and over, "what is your name?" How often have I misunderstood what someone is asking me or telling me about their house? How many times have I been oblivious to this misunderstanding?

MA: A SENSE OF PLACE

The Japanese concept *Ma* might help explain how a place can become a good one and where a "sense of place" came from. A German architect, Nitschke, explains *Ma* in an article published in Japan Architect in 1966. He begins the article by describing in detail the ideogram the Japanese have for *Ma* and where it comes from.

In Nitschke's "key to understanding of Japanese concepts of planning" he goes on to explain that put together, the two parts of the ideogram for *Ma* "suggest moonlight peeping through chinks in a doorway."

[A]n element of time is implied in addition, since space and time are considered as related and relative entities, neither are fixed. They are taken as *Ku*, empty, not having a nature of their own. Thus *Ma* in the Japanese sense has many levels of meaning—it is beyond and yet includes the concept of three dimensional form and space—it has a connotation of time in that an event may serve to define a place—it is of a subjective nature, stimulated from without by the disposition of symbols, whether they be tangible forms and visibly defined spaces or those created by movement and happenings.(Nitschke, 1966, 116).

I spent one Easter at Pearl Beach on the Central Coast of NSW lying like the photographer Max Dupain's "Sunbaker" with my hands under my chin, nose pointed into the sand, reading an article on *ma*. It was the only reading matter I had taken with me so I could not escape it.

It was a long article. I lay in the blazing sun, a golden expanse of beach around me filled with other people doing much the same as myself—sunbaking, sleeping or reading.

The article seemed to make no sense to me. Every concept associated with *ma* seemed difficult. I am not certain I ever got to its end. It remained with me, though, and on re-reading it decades later, I thought it explained a lot about how to think about places, particularly good ones.

Nitschke had difficulty finding appropriate words to explain "unfamiliar states of consciousness" and he decided it would be best to coin new words rather than confuse the issue by using "existing ones with their associations." He was very explicit in setting out definitions:

> I speak of space in the traditional Western three-dimensional sense—the obverse of substantial, tangible objects. As a box viewed from the outside is an object, so the inside is space.
>
> According to Giedion, Western consciousness of space as revealed in its architecture at any period is directly related to the comprehension of science and mathematics current at that particular time (Nitschke, 1966, 117).

However,

> The traditional Japanese consciousness of space is totally different from that of a time/space theory... Space was never understood as a physical factor (in Japan). The Japanese sense of space is *ma*, best described as a consciousness of place, not in the sense of a "piazza", an enclosed three-dimensional entity, but rather as Hans Scharoun used the word Platz in his first Berlin competition scheme, where he spoke of Zentrale Platze or places of central activities.

Hence,

> I feel...that the English word *place* could be used to imply the simultaneous awareness of the intellectual

concepts form + space, object + space, coupled with subjective experience. In this way, we can get a bit nearer to the Japanese concept of space, which, from now on, I will refer to as a sense of place, or simply *ma*. So—this Japanese sense of *ma* is not something that is created by compositional elements; it is the thing that takes place in the imagination of the human who experiences these elements. Therefore, one could define *ma* as "experiential" place, being nearer to mysterious atmosphere caused by the external distribution of symbols (Nitschke, 1966, 117).

Even if we are unable to define what a "good place" is, most of us have had the experience of one.

Consider the veranda. In Australia, we generally think there is something intrinsically good about a veranda; it makes a good place. It is something you want to add to your house. A veranda is an in-between place between outside place and inside place where you can do both inside and outside activities.

A veranda has certain requirements, though, which aren't always included in their actual design. A veranda needs to be wide enough for a table with chairs on either side of it so you can sit inside/outside with friends or family and have a meal. When you are not eating at the table you might paint there, and because the table is outside on the veranda, it doesn't matter so much if paints goes everywhere.

A veranda needs to be wide enough for a bed so you can lie on it, be outside and not feel as though you are slovenly. When the sun-drenched bed lures you to sleep after reading for a while, you might wake to find it has started raining. You listen to the sound of the rain on the metal roof as you lie there in your in-between state.

A veranda also needs to be wide enough to protect the rest of the house, the inside, from the devastating summer sun or from the winds. A veranda is a wonderful thing!

Yet most verandas are no longer like this. Most verandas are not made with *ma*. They don't consider either place or time. Their dimensions are mean. They are not wide enough for the bed to sleep in on steamy nights, nor for the table to sit around and have a meal. What has been forgotten is that a veranda is more than simply a thing to be checked off a list. It once had actual functional value. More and more frequently, verandas are not good places. Nitschke might say they have no ma. Still, we have a collective belief based on the memory of their past *ma*.

The concept of *ma* as an experiential place seems closer to my understanding of how many Aboriginal people experience Country, land, and place, and why suburban brick veneer houses seem to be so inappropriate. The houses placed upon Country for Aboriginal peoples have no good imaginings associated with them. This is the case no matter what their orientation, and no matter how they are placed on lots in streets laid out with little consideration for anything other than expediency of construction and proximity to existing or future infrastructure. These streets disrupt the paths of the Dreaming and Songlines. They take no account of ceremony, or of who is permitted to see whom or what, nor of time.

These streets and houses have no experiential place; in fact, quite the opposite, they have been laid out with no understanding of the place where they have been dumped. They add nothing to the experience of being in a place; they do not elevate how one might experience the place. Their placements are random and meaningless.

Ma isn't like feng shui, with universal rules. It is more, as Nitschke says, a "sense" of things. It takes experience, intuition and a love of the place to give a place *ma*.

In a section titled "Sophisticated Order" Nitschke talks about one of the systems the Japanese use to make good places and construct *ma*. This system is diagonal planning, "one of Japan's most unique creations."

> Diagonal planning permits new elements, of the same or different quality and size, to be added or taken away as required. In other words, it permits change—growth, fulfilment and decay. One is reminded that the Chinese/Japanese character for change, *eki*, also stands for "ease." Each phase of growth is complete and beautiful in itself, nothing seems to be missing. The eternal architectural paradox, that of giving an impression of completeness within incompleteness, is solved. "Life itself silently solves this paradox all the time, a human, an animal and tree does not at any stage suggest visual incompleteness" (Nitschke, 1966, 133).

This seems to me to be appropriate as a planning tool for all housing, and for Aboriginal housing in particular. Aboriginal peoples usually have a very strong consciousness of place. It seems to me that Japanese-style diagonal plans, which have the potential to grow and open up continuously to change and to nature, might be a good model for Aboriginal housing. Such plans allow for surveillance yet at the same time provide privacy and multiple entry points. There can be distance between people rather than have everyone jammed together. Diagonal plans allow for small courtyards with views framing Country. Views change as you walk through the house and you are always close to outside—and with a veranda you are always both indoors and outdoors.

Ma, I believe, means openness, constant change and a relationship to nature and Country.

Dimensions and Ma

Maybe one reason Aboriginal people are unhappy with their houses is that the houses they are given are ugly— not only because they are broken down and small, but because they are mean in size and demeanor.

How did this happen? Was it done deliberately?

In Australia, people generally want their house to be made of brick—usually of clay extruded brick rather than concrete block or the more expensive clay pressed brick. You can tell the difference between the two kinds of clay bricks by holes—an extruded brick has regular small holes through it and a dry pressed brick has a hollow in its top, called the frog. In Australia, clay and concrete bricks are different in dimensions and proportions, so if you were to run out of clay bricks for a project and someone gave you some concrete ones, they wouldn't fit together. Both types of bricks are different in size from any of the sheeting materials. Each sheeting material has its own individual set of dimensions. Tiles, carpet and vinyl come in different lengths and widths as well. And what about windows? You name it. Each manufacturer will have a slightly different sheet size or unit size from the one detailed in the brochure you hold in your hand. Everything will require cutting.

The sheet proportions are ugly. The standard window is ugly. This no doubt explains why the Australian house is so awkward and ugly. No matter which material or window you purchase, each is as ugly as its neighbor. Many small ugly parts can only make up a large (and most Australian houses *are* large) ugly building.

The inherent ugliness of each material is in part why an architect is unwilling to use standard materials. As a result, in an architect designed building, everything has to be cut or re-shaped or made anew so it will not be ugly. Everything has to be made specially—every window and door, everything. Time is needed to do this reshaping, and of course time is money.

It is, therefore, only wealthy people who can afford to build a house with an architect and to have the custom designed and custom made materials and fittings. I don't understand this, since wealthy people tend to spend less time at home and more time travelling and swanning around from place to place. Those who can't afford a house, on the other hand, have to stay at home pretty much all the time.

This seems a shame. Surely, even if you aren't wealthy, you might still deserve to live in a beautiful place. Perhaps you have even more need of a beautiful place, given that not everything else may be going so smoothly. If every building material was shaped around the Golden Mean, as Le Corbusier tried to do, maybe every building could be beautiful. Every space could be a place.

Having achieved a world in which every space was a place, we could move onto other questions.

During my architectural education, there was virtually no discussion as to what might make a place a "place"—or, more importantly, what might make a place a good one. A sense of place was spoken about, although I never did understand why it was a "sense" of place we were after rather than simply a place. After all, we speak of a room, not a sense of a room.

A sense of place was one of those ideas where it was always assumed you understood what was being spoken of, and to ask the question, "What is the sense of place?" you risked expulsion from the inner circle.

TRANSLATING MEASUREMENT

Le Corbusier was a Modernist architect who wanted there to be a language for architecture. He wanted there to be a proper system. He wanted there to be a sense of proportion. He wanted there to be consistency. He wanted architecture to refer to the Golden Mean. He believed that good buildings would fix just about everything. In short, he wanted to create a new order.

Le Corbusier's Modulor system of measurement would be used by all building products and processes. Then all products could easily be mixed and matched. He felt that if proportion and the Golden Mean could guide the measurement of each product, using them together in building a building would mean the building too would be well proportioned.

His vision was one architecture—in fact, one world—with everything ruled by the Golden Mean. Of course there was actually only one person in the world who could handle this type of project, and it was himself, Le Corbusier.

He had researched this quite a lot. He had looked at what currently existed and found that there were myriad systems of scale and dimensions. He pooled these together, analyzed them, laid them next to each other, stood them up and knocked them over one by one, and then re-assessed them and melded them into the one grand scheme, The Modulor.

Amongst other things, his new system resolved two of the major systems: the Imperial and the Metric, which had been fighting each other for time immemorial.

The Imperial system with its feet and inches came out of an intimate knowledge of the body and nature. Its strange, ever-changing measurements glided between countries, slipping and tripping over one another, defining and re-defining themselves. Measuring required an education. Division had to be made by unruly numbers like sixteen, three, fourteen, five thousand two hundred and twenty-eight, to name a few. The forged metal measures representing the inch, the foot, and the yard were lost in the Great Fire of London and had to be re-defined. But this was after American Independence. The colonists had sailed off with the older measures in hand and preferred to keep them. As a result, there were two inter-related measuring systems—the Imperial System as spelt out in the 1824 UK Weights and Measures Act, and the USA system. They met only at the base, where the human meets the ground: at the foot—not the foot length but the body in shoe sizes, counting backwards from the barleycorn, thirteen in all.

The history of the Imperial system is embedded in each word which makes every measurement an adventure. The poppy seed. The barleycorn. The stick. The foot. The yard. The furlong. The league.

The relationship diagram is rhizomic, wild. It looks more Deleuze and Guatarri than they could imagine. If they had not been steeped already in the Metric system, it is possible they would have had to invent it.

With the shoe on the other foot, the Metric system is a scientific system, based on decimals, based on facts, based on an absolute. The meter, from the Greek meaning "measure," was a highly definitive measurement, ascertained to be one ten-millionth of the length of the earth's meridian along a quadrant— or make that the length of a pendulum having a half-period of one second—or was that 1,000,000 / 0.643 846 96 wavelengths in air of the red line of the cadmium spectrum—or maybe, 1,650 763.73 wavelengths in vacuum of the radiation corresponding to the transition between levels 2p10 and 5d5 of the krypton-86 atom—or even (sounding good) the length travelled by light in a vacuum during 1/299,792,458 of a second.

No matter, it is exact and it is held as a brass bar of metal, cast to exactly this length (whatever it may be) and then used as a constant standard—although the bar is now platinum—better really if it is platinum-iridium and held at a constant (although even this is subject to change as more and more exactness is sought) temperature.

Fact over fiction.

Truth over Narrative.

Science over Imperialism.

Unfortunately, this exact, scientific metric system wasn't enough for Corb. He started working on his own system at the same time as Einstein was re-conceptualizing time. Einstein commented on The Modulor (or so Corb claims): "making the bad difficult and the good easy" (Corbusier, mcmliv 5).

Corb failed to have noticed any systems outside of the European, for example, the system the Japanese had developed. The Japanese internal sizing of rooms was based on the tatami, a thick straw mat originally used for sitting but also possible to sleep on. Many of the sheet materials—plywood for example—were similar in size to the tatami mat, so a more wholistic system was already available.

The tatami mat is approximately the size of a person. It can be shifted and carried by a single person. It is 6' by 3' (180 by 90 cm) but this varies marginally from region to region. A room can be described by the number of mats on its floor. A room might be a four and a half mat room (the traditional size of a Tea Ceremony Room) or six tatami mat room in size. This allows an easy imagining of the size of the room. There are auspicious and inauspicious ways to lay out the tatami, and one's future, or lack thereof, may depend on this.

The system Corb developed was based on the height of a man with one arm stretched above his head, the other resting on a benchtop. This was the basic unit. This man was based on himself, which would have been fine except that Corbusier was a small man and most other men were quite a bit bigger. When Corb was criticized for this oversight he developed another Modulor based on these other, larger men. Thus within a few years, he had two systems of the Modulor—a blue series and a red one.

You would be correct at this point to wonder if it had even occurred to Corb to imagine that women might be using some of this architecture—the occasional kitchen, bathroom, bedroom or public space, for example. And thus that there might be a third or even a fourth series based on the small woman and the larger one. And this is a question I asked myself, but decided to silence.

So much of my architectural education came about because I wanted what all my compatriots wanted because I wanted to be a part of them.

If only, Corbusier thought, he could get a system that aligned proportional measurement and the Golden Section—Aahhh, the Golden Section, the Golden Mean—and years later in architecture school, Aahhhh we all sighed—and no one stopped to ask what this might be—then we could have universal standardization....

(And then, Corb must have muttered, rubbing his hands together, and then I could make my fortune at last. I would have the right to claim royalties on everything that is constructed on the basis of this measuring system....)

But it never happened. We students entered the world struggling with brick rods and thumbing through endless catalogues to find what we were looking for, something that would match what we were thinking of, or what we hoped at least would work. We drew painstakingly by hand, learning slowly the trade of drafting and becoming immersed in the world of rotring pens, different grades of paper, lead clutch pencils, razor blades, a myriad of different things to know about just to begin.

But those concerns, so all-consuming at the time, have disappeared and now I, like so many others, no longer can help the new students. Now with computer-aided drafting it is easy to copy from one drawing to the next—or so the theory goes; the practice is not so straightforward.

Ma and House

A place may seem empty but the ghosts, spirits, entities still live there. Is *ma* still there? Of course! They appear in Dreamings.

Communities are imprisoned in an in-between place, knowing where their place is but unable to get there, imprisoned sometimes on a small island of their original land, a part of their *ma*, sometimes all of it. It is as if they have downed tools and sat down at the spot where they did so, and have been unable to move any further.

Being stopped from wandering is one thing, but then to be stuffed into a box, a small hot dwelling, a house with little cross ventilation, no insulation, a small noisy air conditioner which is expensive to run, a low ceiling, with flimsy hollow core doors, and little covered outdoor area, is another thing entirely. A dwelling can produce more problems than it solves but this is the only thing ever offered.

At times, in some communities, there are requirements that certain people are not to be seen by others for cultural reasons. Houses by their nature draw people together, force them to be together, and can make it difficult to avoid those who ought to be avoided. Complicated arrangements of doors to get around this problem are needed.

Escape must be possible from everywhere at any time. A house of escape is barely a house at all, for there is nowhere to sit without the threat of being interrupted, a door opening and banging into you as you try to get on with whatever it is you are doing.

Those doing Aboriginal housing try to accommodate this, try to do the best they can, but the solutions are pretty much the same.

When is a house not a house?

A house is a house is a house, even if it is a house in an Aboriginal or Torres Strait Islander community.

Sometimes it has seemed to me it would be better to simply make a good ablutions block. Once people no longer live a nomadic lifestyle, the removal of waste and access to clean water are essential but maybe the house-bit—the bedrooms, living room and dining room are not needed. A good ablutions block and a common laundry for washing clothes; a big kitchen where there is room for butchering meat and cleaning fish and later having a big meal with anyone who is around might work. Perhaps a few caravans could provide a cosy place to sleep and each one of these able to be moved to include changing alliances and the rules about who can see whom at different times.

Not everywhere. Just some places, just sometimes, just maybe.

MA AI — 間合い

There is another type of *ma* that is part of a sense of place which is different again.

When I begin aikido, a twentieth century martial art that is based on the blending of forces rather than on using force against force, I come face to face with this ma. Aikido is different to most other martial arts in that it is almost always practised with someone else. It is difficult to practice alone. It uses concepts such as "blending" and "flow", with one person taking the role of "attacker" and the other taking the role of "defender." But the roles are not quite so clear cut in practice.

In aikido, *ma ai* is crucial for being able to work out how close you ought to be to someone. *Ma ai*, the distance or the place between people, changes as the people change—tall, short, long armed, short armed and so forth. It is about "relationship" and refers to "proper distance" the space from, or position in relation to, an attacker but it includes the idea of maintaining a sense of harmony between attacker and defender.

In aikido I find it harder to work with someone who is taller than me, just as they find it hard to work with me since I am so small and therefore close to them. To stay out of their long reach I can move further away or contrary to all intuition, get much closer. This allows me to reach them more easily and means they are cramped. This distance, this *ma ai*, is a place of negotiation and relationship.

> In its simplest sense, *ma ai* is the space that allows you to be safe. But *ma ai* changes as an attack occurs. While you don't want to be standing within your partner's sphere of influence before an attack (since here you can easily strike and be hit), once the attack occurs, your relationship (your *ma ai*) changes dramatically. Because aikido responses almost always use blending, entering, or turning, you will find yourself very close to your partner. Don't panic! In aikido, as in love, close is good (Borg, n.d.)

It is the sense of flow and oneness I seek when doing aikido, but I rarely find it.

I practice aikido in a class of only men, who are taller, broader, and stronger than me, and although in aikido strength is not meant to play a part, the truth is that until you are technically proficient, using strength makes a technique easier. Early on, if you do not have sufficient strength to overpower your opponent, you get frustrated. You have to settle yourself and commit to practicing and practicing, to make sure you get your technique down.

I am drawn to aikido. I do try to make sure my technique is good. I also try to make my techniques flow.

But in reality I usually fail to have any real skill in aikido. Sometimes, rarely, I do an aikido technique and I do enter the flow. It is difficult to explain in any detail exactly what I mean by this, but suddenly I have done a technique without thinking or worrying about it and everything happens smoothly. It is a feeling that everything is natural, a feeling of being at home in the movement.

It is the exact same feeling I have standing in red dirt.

Time stops but it is also speeding past. The technique finishes and then I am back to being a stranger again, standing on an alien land, all angles and awkwardness, struggling to do the next one.

It takes years to become a good aikido-ka and there is always more to know. As a beginner you have no idea of the subtlety in a technique.

People talk of the extension of body in place and time, of egolessness, of being able to deal equally with a variety of different sizes and types of people, of welcoming people in to yourself, of initiating action before it is needed.

Perhaps my technique in aikido is not being present.

"Look at me. Look at me. Look me in the eyes," my aikido teacher says as I try to apply the wrist pin to his arm.

The pin is meant to hold him, hurt him, control him.

I don't want to be doing this. I don't understand why I would want to hurt someone, except that I am trying to learn this martial art.

"You must look at me so you can see when the pin takes affect and you know when to stop, otherwise you will really hurt me," the aikido teacher says.

I don't want to see the pain in his eyes. Besides, what if I can't do it, what if I never even vaguely hurt him so the pain never comes, what then?

So I pretend not to be there, and instead I look away, pretending I am over there away from this and doing something else entirely.

The light is very beautiful outside, over there, at this time of night. The small room we do the aikido class in, the dojo, has glass windows beginning at a height of three feet (one meter) on three sides; the fourth side has photos of aikidoka past and present, including a photo of the founder, O'Sensei. The room has a pointed roof and, from inside, the structure is clearly visible. It is like a small glasshouse for hot-house plants, but instead of plants, it is we who practice aikido, we aikidoka, who are being hot-housed. We are being tested mentally, watching to see each other's cracks which always come when you least expect or want them.

The dojo is painted white and set in the expansive gardens of a park. Across the way I can see the sun setting beyond the oval. I think how glorious….

But I cannot escape into the other "there" of the park. The teacher is the master and I am the student— and more than this, I am a woman and he is a man and although this is meant to be a place of learning, we all know it is just like the rest of life. If push comes to shove, he will shove me and it won't matter if I have looked into his eyes and seen his pain, because he will have hurt me first.

The realities of life are mirrored in everything we do. Pressed, I might snap and hold the pin hard in anger, look with hatred into his eyes and not let go. But I am already the only woman in the class. I already have the numbers stacked against me. So I hang my head—dog-like, foolish, not doing as I am told, not explaining why I am not doing as I am told—sullen, difficult, resistant. These are the only tools I have to defeat him.

I am sitting in a place of *ma*, or as you say in aikido, in *ma ai*—the relationship between me and others, me and the writing here. In aikido, you are always in relationship with something, mostly someone else. *Ma ai* is more than *ma*. *Ma ai* is the space between an "us," you and me—a space that varies, depending on us. There are also words for a "large space or distance between the two of us"—*to ma*; "a single step between the two of us"—*itto ma* and "a small distance between the two of us," where I am/you are already into the other person's space, *chika ma*,

I know how much space to leave around me to feel comfortable as I walk along a street or how to leave enough space between me and the person in front when I stand in a queue in a shop. Starting in aikido, I have to learn to re-negotiate this space of in between. When my space meets your space, we need to work together and find where each of us begins and ends. This is the beginnings of understanding *ma ai*. Over time, I hope that this will become a natural sense but until then, each time I have to try and sort it out- along with all the other parts of the aikido movement I am trying to do.

I am here in relationship to you but also with you. I can declare one way or the other who I am, who I want to be, who I choose to be, who I choose not to be. To make a choice in these and act on one of them, I risks losing the other possibilities.

At times, I enjoy being in a position of not knowing for certain.

In this not-knowing, there is possibility.

In this not-knowing, I can be everything.

Kannagara no michi
(Way of the gods)

Organs huge as continents:
Connective tissues as tree roots
Pulled up beyond snapping point
Stretched, polished, transcended -
Walk tall, sacred being!
Cross the floating bridge of heaven
Over the serene mountain lake.
Feel your centre leave the ground
Look down into the shining waters -
ruffled with flat green leaves,
white lotus flowers, golden centres afloat ,
dragon flies shimmering there.

Look up past the yellow fringed clouds
through their airy depths
Into a starry formless field
Notice how you vibrate, move through, reach out,
Gather up, gather in, gather round
Roots dangling rootless
Mouth open toothless
Head thrown back, lips open wide, gulping
Earth is already lost to you.
Spiralling into infinity
You will be greeted on the other shore
In the pure land of Monju.

...To go on foot and do one's own work is the best road to strength and health. (The Hojoki, 19)

TRANSLATING *HITO* AND *SU*

人

Rejoice over
the purling of a stream
reward the many people you've met
they've denied themselves space.

This character, 人, is a kanji—English text *hito*; translation—"man."

I had seen *hito* before and remembered it represented a person walking. Maybe I had been told this or assumed it because that is how she looks, a quiet person taking herself out on a stroll around the text, legs separated, body upright, arms tucked to her sides.

There is a slight leaning back from tiredness or exhaustion even—maybe she has recently finished a long walk, maybe a pilgrimage even, and feels happy, whistling softly to herself as she nears home once more.

She pops up here, there and everywhere, all over the text as though she were searching for something or someone—her next of kin, perhaps.

In my first translation I removed all trace of her throughout the text and replaced her with a photo. It was a photo of a caterpillar-shaped hole in a fence behind which was a truck depot. The photo was one I took in

Alice Springs. Alice Springs is *yipirinya* (caterpillar) Country. The fence is painted dirt red below and clay yellow above the cut. There is a brilliant sky above the fence. In the gap between the red and yellow, the trucks of the depot are visible.

Something didn't work with this photo though. It needed an introduction. Everyone who enters a community needs to introduce themselves to the Traditional Owners and Elders so they can welcome you to their Country and connections can be made and certainty built. If I was going to replace hito, I needed to introduce them around to everyone first. It led me to wonder about my own place in the text and in life and to realize I have been removing myself from the world, destroying the evidence, sometimes leaving clues, but leaving no identifying marks. "Tread lightly on the earth," someone said.

I have a similar uneasiness wondering if I am or am not who I think I am. It has run through most of my life, just like the possibility of being or not being Aboriginal.

Perhaps my "Aboriginal" nature is only a motif, like the fence of this truck depot, alluding to something about which I am not clear, or something that has been put on as camouflage for tourists.

Or perhaps my need for an Aboriginal heritage is similar to the desire of those who yearn for this identification, who want the skin name, the identification of "otherness", "specialness."

The story of my (s)kin remains un(re)coverable.

I remember my grandmother saying, "I'm a little Aborigine."

Her skin is very dark.

"A gypsy, a gypsy," my mother insists.

The other family members rush to silence my grandmother, to place a tea towel over her head and pretend she is not there.

My grandfather says, "Your grandmother is from the other side of the tracks." He nods and taps the side of his nose knowingly.

"Mum's the word," he says.

When I tell this to my mother later, she says it is very bad of him to say that. She doesn't say it isn't true. To admit to being Aboriginal during most of Australia's colonized history would be a total "shame job." People avoided this truth as much as possible. To be almost anything else was preferable. "A touch of the tar brush" was enough to banish you from the mainstream. If you have hidden something like this for most of your life and have read the propaganda of the press which continues to malign Aboriginal peoples, writing only ever in deficit about them, it is hard to be honest about this. I know of sisters with the same mother and father where one will identify as an Aboriginal woman and the other will not.

My cousin says her mother (my mother's sister) was always spoken of at school as the "gin" and in the end, my cousin asked her not to pick her up from school anymore.

We play card games only Aboriginal people know.

We have relatives we never see. Uncle Aub arrives in the dark. He stands at the door behind the thick insect screen and refuses to come in, despite our urging him to enter. "He's very dark," my grandmother calls from the kitchen. "He doesn't like people to see him." He leaves things at the door—dried apricots, oranges—for us to find in the morning.

The fingers all point in one direction, the lips mouth "yes", the heads shake deliberately "no."

I was always good at picking up double signals.

When I start doing work in Aboriginal communities, I find myself pushed to the front while everyone else from the Department lurks at the door, covering their faces, smirking. In community after community the people ask me where I come from. In community after community I answer that I am from the Department of Housing.

Everybody laughs.

In the beginning, I wonder what is funny.

Thinking about this, the truck depot fence photo I was going to use for the translation began to seem flippant.

HERMANNSBURG

Perhaps it is not the "I" everyone else sees that I want to remove, but the history I am made up of—this shadowy family of mine that long ago inserted itself into a landscape in which it did not belong.

My great great great grandfather and his flock of three thousand sheep inserted themselves into the country around Hermannsburg by walking there and destroying thousands of years of lifestyle. He did this and made way for me who would later make way for houses. He seems never to have got to belonging here. He left it to me to translate his place back into the text.

I visited Hermannsburg with a group of Aboriginal people. I remember little now of the visit. Perhaps it was the heat. Perhaps it was the long journey there. I have seen it happen to other people, this lethal combination whereby they simply lose themselves, do not know themselves, when they arrive in the middle of the desert.

But there he is, my great great great grandfather, hanging on the wall in the museum at Hermannsburg. I hadn't expected it. I walked into the single room of the museum to look around half wanting, half not wanting to find him, and there he was. I didn't make it up. I have seen his portrait.

Memory is fragments of stories without end, coincidences and fatal landings. Memory is made new in each remembrance. Versions that could be true or could be false. They all contribute. The version delivered in the anecdote is embellished for effect, to bring the memory to life (Prosser, 2009).

I pointed my grandfather out to the Aboriginal fellow next to me. I was excited.

"That's my great great great grandfather," I said.

In every photo I find of my great great great grandfather he looks extremely severe. He always wears a hat. In one photo it is a strange hat with a broad band around his forehead and a triangular piece on top of this. His hands are folded. His beard looks like a false one attached by elastic bands over his ears. His mouth is pursed. The women on either side of him lean in ever so slightly. Every photo focuses on him; the others next to him are slightly blurry.

The words blurted out. "That's my great great great grandfather."

Everyone stopped their chatter and looked at me. I was strangely excited and proud, not of what he did, but of the conviction of his beliefs, at his tenacity in getting to this place.

I looked into the portrait's eyes.

I was suddenly no longer there. I never wanted to be there at all. I wanted to back pedal quickly and deny the relationship.

I was ashamed.

I did not see a likeness, but is this because there is no likeness or because even if there were a likeness, I would not want to see it? I was a pious child who wrote poems to God and imagined talking with Him. Perhaps that was my likeness.

Because I do see myself in a photo of Aboriginal people at Hermannsburg I come across much later. The photo is of women and babies. The older women look despondent, resigned. Some of the younger girls still have curiosity in their eyes and are squinting into the camera. Everyone is wearing the same striped sack-like dresses, three buttons at the top, shapeless. The trees conceal some of the taller women, or perhaps they are deliberately hiding in them. The younger ones at the front are jostling for a position in front of the camera.

The girls in the absolute front row have their hands clasped in front of them, all except one. This girl has her arms folded in front of her. Her head is at a slight angle. Her mouth is clenched. Her hair has been tossed back behind her ears.

Wat r yew lookin at? Arsehole. What yew think yer playing at?

She hates the photographer. She hates the striped pinny she has been forced to wear. She hates being here. She hates you looking at her. She hates me looking at her. She hates being told what to do. She hates the whole fuckin' lotta yer.

This is not me, although I would like to say it is. I am the girl standing next to her. She is a slightly shorter girl. She has blond hair. She is half burrowed behind the girl with the folded arms. Her head is tilted down, her eyes only slightly lifted to half-see what is about to happen. Only one arm is showing fully, the fingers of the other arm just peeping as it holds the other arm.

This one looks like me.

She is the one who will later get into trouble for not looking into the eyes of her aikido teacher.

Look at me. Look at me. Look into my eyes. Let me control you.

I bought a painting at Hermannsburg. Everyone thought it looked gloomy. It hung on the wall in my house behind the piano so no one except me would see it. I remember the colors as dark and dirge-like but also strong and defiant. But when I pull it out from where it has fallen, I find my memory of it is wrong. It does have a dark dung-colored background, but over this are yellow ochre and khaki green dots as well as tiny deep full-bodied red ones that contrast brilliantly against the other colors. There is a strong diagonal through the painting. The corners are cut off by representations of thick banana fruit vines.

It is a women's painting and shows women working together. The women sit under the sky, an arc of stars and the moon moving over them. Each woman has her tools laid out around her. Each is working independently and yet they are together. The red dots are scattered around them—points of conflict between them perhaps.

I wanted a painting that represented my journey to Hermannsburg—the first time I had visited Central Australia with a mob of Aboriginal people—my first time to see the place my great great great grandfather followed his calling.

This painting shows movement—a spiral into, then out of, a center.

I am the center.

Everyone else is sitting around looking to me. "Your move," they say.

You can be held here in the center of it all or move on out if you so choose. It reflects my swirl of emotions there. Yet it has me sitting alongside other women.

I met and then lost a sister in Central Australia—not a blood sister but one to whom I am connected by life. When I found her again it was as though we had never gone missing. The return visit with her was too fast for me to fully take it in.

I tried to text her, forgetting telephone signals can be weak and flukey in remote locations.

I chose the truck depot/caterpillar photograph to replace 人 when I first began my translating. It is the sort of photo one might expect for Aboriginal communities and in hindsight it was never suitable. The photo is brightly colored and represents a Dreaming I know little about.

I see that the photo would never do.

Heimat

After my father died, my mother and I decided to reverse great great great grandfather's journey and return to the

Heimatland. We were not clear what it was we might be searching for—just as he had no idea what he might find.

We traveled to Tiefenort, Germany where he came from. We had no expectations or knowledge of the place. Mum spoke no German despite having been brought up in a small South Australian German town where, even after a century, many continue to speak German.

As a twenty-year-old I had gone to Germany and visited a commune where they made Bach Flower Remedies. I had wanted to stay on a commune in Germany for a long time.

It was a difficult place to get to. I had written asking if I could visit and stay for a while. The residents had replied warmly but when I arrived, they were anything but warm. I stayed in a room where I could hear the river. The river ran through my head all day and night. I sat on the floor on the mattress in the room I had been given and felt lonely and uncomfortable.

This commune dream was a disaster. I was not certain what I was seeking but it wasn't this. I left after a few days.

The next time I went to Germany was when my mother and I journeyed to the village from which my great great great grandfather came to Australia. I wanted Tiefenort to be my place.

My mother arrived before me and found us space in the attic of a hotel on the main street of Erfurt, from which we could travel to Tiefenort. The trams below the window rattled past in ten-minute intervals. Despite the cold, we set out almost immediately for Eisenach, the next closest place to Tiefenort we could locate.

Everyone was extremely helpful in the Tourist Office and explained the same small details over and over. But that was the only information they could give. Some had heard of Tiefenort but no one knew how we might get there.

We peered nervously out of the window as the train took us to Eisenach.

We had no plans beyond Eisenach—no idea as to where Tiefenort was in relation to it nor how we might get there. But when we hopped off the train at Eisenach Station, there was a bus stop and standing at the front of the line of buses was one saying "Tiefenort." It was a miracle.

Before we had time to think, we were on board and heading for Tiefenort. My mother was elated now, chattering about the scenery as we passed, wondering whether this or that would have been there when great great great grandfather was there. It was exciting. Everything took on meaning. The road wound backwards and forwards merrily along a small river of greyish water, the bowed trees trailing leaves in its shallows.

I had spoken to the driver as we got on and hoped I had explained we wanted to get off at Teifenort. In the strange way tourists do, I also explained many superfluous things—my mother's age, the recent death of my father, my mother's relationship to Germany and Tiefenort and how we had managed to get this far. I was worried I had succeeded in explaining nothing like this at all and so I made sure I was alert to any sign that might arise and show us we were there.

Finally, the bus driver leant out and signaled to us from the front of the bus.

Hier. He pointed to the floor of the bus.
Wir halten hier.
It must be Teifenort.

The road was muddy and wet. It was extremely cold. We had on our gloves and hats and as many articles of clothing as we could muster. We stepped out of the bus into Tiefenort—deep place or deep north, depending on where you hyphenate the word.

My mother still goes on and on about it. And I guess it was strange. As we landed on the sacred ground of Tiefenort, the bells of a church began to ring. And my mother began to cry.

The bus left us in a smallish space with a road leading into it and then on the other side, out of it again. There were small houses on both sides of the street with timber structure and lathe lining It was almost a square but with little precision nor any obvious reason for its shape.

We followed the sound of the bells up a steep icy slope. We hesitated at the noticeboard in front of the church, which was set back farther from the road. I attempted to read out what the notices said was happening at the church over the coming week. I was expecting to see his name, our name, somewhere on the board, proving we still belonged here.

As I read slowly, translating in my schoolgirl German into English for my mother, the bells stopped. A man then emerged from the church. He asked in German what we were looking for. I told him we were there because it was my mother's 80th birthday and she wanted to see her ancestor's home. I couldn't explain in my broken German that I was also searching for something else— something I was not clear about. When I told him we were Heidenreichs, he nodded immediately. He knew the name and took us into the church to show us where it was engraved on the walls of the church and written into the church records. This was our church. It was the very same bells our relative would have heard ringing. We were home.

We got to talking, my mother excitedly going on and on in English, prompting me to say this and then that. It was quickly evident the German bellringer understood no English. With my mother babbling in one ear and the German bellringer in the other, I became ever more confused. Most of the German words I should have known disappeared.

I think I understood what he was saying to me but I was unable to say in English to my mother what it was, nor to respond to him in German. The whole lot was broken—my German, my English, the conversation—so I started to make up things which approximated roughly what I thought was being said to me. My mother continued in English, asking me to tell him this and the other—as though it were in fact my great great great-grandfather we were talking to rather than the bellringer on the street in a small German village.

The bellringer wanted to take us somewhere. I thought he was saying he knew the last Heidenreich who lived in the village and he would show us where he lived. He began to walk cautiously down the icy, slippery hill. The cold was rapidly changing the snow on the road into black ice which glistened as we gingerly followed the man down the hill. He was still talking in German to me and pointing things out, telling me all sorts of stories about this and that Heidenreich and other things, little of which I could understand. I tried desperately to keep my mind on his German words. It was mainly words, not constructed sentences I was hearing. Word order I knew it to be extremely important in German but I heard only nouns, not clauses, phrases or even verbs. I responded by repeating and pointing towards myself, or somewhere else, or at the same thing over and over as we all struggled down the cobbled hill.

At the bottom of the hill, the German bellringer stopped and waved his right arm at a corner. On one side of the corner was an old derelict house of traditional construction. Its windows were partly broken, partly boarded up. The curtains were dusty. It appeared to have been standing empty like this for a long time. On the corner opposite, there was a vacant lot. What he explained, or what I think he explained, was this vacant lot was where my great great great grandfather lived, or was born, or the Heidenreichs had abandoned, in the early part of the twentieth century. Maybe it was where the last Heidenreich lived, or maybe the last Heidenreich he knew about had lived here. Sometime comparatively recently, the house had been demolished. But it was a special place, one known by all in Teifenort.

He spoke at length of this place. We stood in the freezing cold, uncertain why we were there, while the man continued to speak. What it seemed to me he said in German was that this site was needed. It had been chosen. It was to be a carpark.

I took a photo of the place. In the photo, a shaft of light descends from the heavens to the corner of this land. At the foot of the shaft of light, there is a small mound. Without this line of light, the mound would never be noticed.

Suddenly, the man had to hurry off and left us there in the cold looking. We stood for a while, my mother and I, and finally moved on to search for a coffee and something to eat. The only place serving meals was open only on weekends and only for dinner. There was a small bakery on the square. We entered and were met by a stony-faced young woman who seemed reluctant for us to eat the rolls we had bought inside her shop although there were empty tables.

Seated in the plastic chairs at the plastic table, we drank the lukewarm coffee. The place was barely warm. It could have been a bakery anywhere. There were no decorations or distinguishing features. The goods the shop sold seemed to have been made in some industrial bakery. The sausage rolls, quiches and pies sat under the fluorescent light and were kept continuously warm, so I knew by the time they were eaten, they would be dry and stale. The stony-faced woman glared at us.

Here we were, finally at home, and we were being made to feel as though we should move on. There was nothing else to see at Tiefenort. No people walked in the streets. No cars drove past. The place began to freeze over again. We returned to the bus stop and waited in the cold for the bus to head back.

That was it: home.

My mum and I did not know ourselves there. We had been erased. We were freezing. Our "place" in Tiefenort was now a car park. I still wonder why they needed a car park.

There is only so long you can stand on a car park and look interested.

JOURNEYS

Hito represents journey, for aren't we all on a journey and now more than ever? The journey to be thin. The journey to be next Australian idol. The journey of the PhD. The journey of life.

There is a long tradition of walking and thinking or at least walking and story-telling. The First Nations' Dreamings would have been spoken of, as people walked through Country and pointed out as people passed through it or sat around the fire at night. The Songlines are part of this.

The way you walk, your stride, the terrain over which you walk, the roll of your foot, the type of shoe you wear, the type of sock and whether it is pulled tight up or whether it has sagged, will affect how easily you think and what it is you think about. Whether your arms are swinging freely or not, whether you are carrying something bulky or heavy—a baby perhaps—or whether you are comfortable or struggling along in pain. It is mesmeric, this walking/thinking, and often it is meditative.

Zen traditions involve walking meditation. You start with your feet and move from the ground upwards feeling into the motion of walking. You feel every part of your foot in its movements. You feel your shin bone and how a slight roll of the foot affects it, or the other way around. You feel your knee, a strange joint meant only to bend but which sometimes twists. Up, up to the top of your head. How it sits up there above the rest, controlling and being controlled. You feel your entire structure. Thinking or not thinking. Being in the here and now.

Every morning I catch the bus into town and walk a kilometer to the office where I work. Most mornings something will occur to me, some important essence of the work I am currently doing. I must write down these essences or else I am likely to forget them entirely. They are fragmented, these thoughts and for them to make any sense at all, I must note down alongside them the book I was reading on the bus into town and a whole range of contextual details.

My most productive thinking seems to be the small space of time between leaving the bus and getting to the first crossing. Here, where I invariably must wait for the lights to change from red to green, something happens—but only if I have let my mind go sufficiently loose, to drift and flutter. Then words, an image, a thought, float to the top, urgent and inspirational, and I dig into my bag to find my phone and with one hand, type in this latest thought.

This fragmented thinking, and then writing, seems part of our times. Everything around us is fragmented—lives, families, friends, dreams, novels, movies, blogs. It is as though we have taken Walter Benjamin's fragmented translation vessel to heart and tried to glue all the pieces into an image. The pieces match in small details but are not necessarily a match in the whole. It is a jig-saw puzzle done without the picture in front of us; we make it up as we go along—make it up into what we want it to be.

It makes no difference whether the pieces fit, because over time we have become good enough at "reading" these fragments and constantly adjusting and amending our idea of what it is we are producing. It is only at completion—at the very end of our lives—we will know what it was we were making.

But despite all my intentional walking, I seem unable to find a good match for what *hito* means to me.

THE HOJOKI RE-MEMBERED

人 has led me astray, over hill and dale, because of my insistence on its removal. It is hard not to want to make each replacement translation deep and rich with meaning. But perhaps it would be better to leave it as simple as possible. Or to leave it and come back to it later.

Perhaps a void best represents me. Because despite searching I find there is little of me to find. And my family continues to be buried.

Su

す

Flames driven by the wind
drifting clouds—little smoke
people complain
what wonder in the Capital!

This character, す is a hiragana—English text *su*; translation—"you."

To you then, *su*—I tried to ignore you, but each time I looked, there you were. Just as each Sunday there is my son at soccer.

Su looked like the running, jumping, soccer playing version of *hito*. But it wasn't—it was *you*.

"You" were always holding me back.

And when I write of "you" I am not clear who "you" are but I know this holding back feeling.

Soccer is such a tricky game. The best team doesn't always win, just as in life. There is the cheating, the falling to the ground pretending to be hurt in order to defer play, the dramatic throwing out and up of arms, the continual loud and raucous battle with the referee,

87

who always favors the other side. When I play soccer, I laugh to remember playing with my son when he was only as high as my hips. He and his friends were so focused that they would run at me and I would end up tripping over them because they were invisible, so small, and I was looking over them at the goal.

Here's *su* running through the text, collecting all and sundry on its way, knocking other things out, driven by the wind and flames.

At the end of the piece, I find a pile high of kanji which *su* has knocked over and pushed to the end. As in life there are people who run amok, and who anticipate that you will too, as you must be the same as them.

I think I would prefer to be one of the loser kanji instead of one of the righteous ones. I would prefer to have done minimal damage on my way.

Given all those with a *su* nature, I am pushed out of the way, because I am not clear who I am or where I come from.

You can take me or leave me.

There is no "body" in the Hojoki. Chomei has taken on the life of a hermit crab with his ten-foot square hut. Like a hermit crab, he is all shell, little body, little heart —mainly head.

When I show the Hojoki to an analyst, he comments that it suggests a man very disappointed with his life. I don't see this and it has worried me that there is something I am missing.

It is true The Hojoki is not a joyous piece but I think it shows someone who is content with what they have—no less, no more.

I am not clear about what I expect, but if this is my endgame, I am not doing it very well. It worries me to write of it. I am not sure how predictive it is. If I write as though this will happen, am I making it actually happen?

The beautiful game, as soccer is called, can be fantastic —fast, close, skilled. Or it can be awful. Sometimes when you watch, it seems nothing is happening. Play is out the back, kicking back to the goalkeeper and playing to the sides, then back again to the goalkeeper with the ball, marking time. It is also flukey. One lapse of concentration. One lucky shot. One mistake and the whole play changes.

Will I reach myself before it is all over? Have I been the best team I can be?

The best friends one can have are flowers and moon, strings and pipe. (The Hojoki, 18)

Translating *Nani*

何

A stern samurai has a boy
who sometimes comes to bear me company
there is nothing to fear

This character, 何, is a kanji—English text *nani*; translation—"what."

It reminds me of a small home. It is definitely a home, not a house, because of its jaunty angle, with everything not quite square. Nor is it symmetrical. There is a little door in the middle. Or maybe it is a window? Or is that a TV? No house can be a real home without a door, without an entry. No house can be a real home without some means of looking out. Nor, surely, can a house be a real home without a TV.

The skillion roof falls down to the west, protecting the rooms on that side from the afternoon sun as every good roof and veranda should. The home is open on the eastern side and this is where the bedrooms will be placed so they will receive the first morning light and everyone can be up bright and early and get themselves ready for school and work. There is a bustling around the house as the occupants rise and shine and in a flurry, they sit down to eat their cornflakes.

Aboriginal people have been moved away from their traditional lifestyles and forced into a colonial, more "settled" lifestyle. Where they used the land in their traditional ways, they were removed from it. Where they used the land the way they were told to use it by white people or the way they saw white people using it, they were removed from it (Goodall, 1996). With no Country, there is little call for people to be getting up early—but it is good to know that if they do need to get up early, the sun will wake them.

When looked at as an elevation drawing, this character looks like a typical 1950s asbestos-cement clad suburban home. When viewed as a plan, it is a protective enclosure with a gap at the front. This protective area is made roughly square from sticks and found objects so the surrounding walls aren't exactly smooth. From inside residents can look out through the gap with a hint of a return, allowing for privacy without being too exclusive. It is like a narrow screen to both conceal and reveal. Within this enclosure there is a small being, feeling comfortable in the space—not too much space but not too little either. The space is just right. It has been made exactly for their needs. It fits like a glove. This small space is exactly like the Hojoki. The little being within the enclosure has their arms outstretched welcoming you into their world. Come in, let me give you a hand.

In my first translation of *nani*, I selected what I thought was a good photo with which to replace the character. It was of a house manipulated to look more like a home than a house. The house had been constructed during the Aboriginal Welfare Board days when houses were made of asbestos cement sheeting and had only a few tiny bedrooms, a minuscule combined living/dining area, a dark kitchen with primitive servicing and minimal facilities. The bathroom was barely wide enough for a person to move crab-like between the shower over the bath to the basin opposite the door. The toilet was separate, a 3' (90 cm) wide corridor space with no window, accessed by walking through a tiny laundry. Everything was there. Everything was mean.

"They should be happy they even have a home," someone at the Social Housing Provider place said.

Many Aboriginal families still live in these houses. They have been their homes now for years. There is a certain pride associated with living in them. Often, they were given to families after a long struggle and now, when the house is really past its use-by date, people are reluctant to leave. It has become home. A larger brick house will be better in many ways but it isn't home; it isn't what someone is used to.

The newer house is arriving too late. It is arriving just as people are getting older and can no longer look after such a large place. It will be much more work. It is better to stay in their tiny asbestos-clad dwelling, which they know and care for.

It was the same for some houses out in western NSW which were primitive in many ways but which represented the first time people had been truly consulted as to how they wanted their houses. The houses were extremely simple with bedrooms off a large living/dining/kitchen area. The bathroom had to be accessed from the outside, via a dirt-floored veranda. When I spoke to people about how to improve their houses, they were extremely protective of them. They wanted things upgraded but did not want the houses removed or changed too significantly. Not everyone responded in this way, but many of the older people did. These people remembered how much effort had gone into getting these houses in the beginning. The struggle and process had been as important as the actual dwelling (Memmott, 1991).

I find this situation hard. Housing comes with a lot of baggage and involves a lot of aspiration. It is not only bricks and mortar. Sometimes a new house is like the first music album you bought after having saved for so long to get it. You look at it now and wonder how on earth you can have been so misguided as to want it. But regardless, you know all its words; you can hum it loudly when called upon to do so. You have a soft spot for it, despite everything.

To visit much of this housing generally involves lengthy travel—hours in a small plane—more hours in a car. When you step out of the car or plane after having travelled for hours, you are hit with a wall of heat and often struck by the squalor. It is easy to jump to a conclusion, based on nothing other than this moment of arrival. What you conclude from what you see is only one facet of the situation.

Deleuze and Guattari would say the situation is not "like a tree" as most people claim, instead it is a rhizome.

A rhizome has no beginning or end; it is always in the middle, between things, interbeing, intermezzo. The tree is filiation, but the rhizome is alliance, uniquely alliance. The tree imposes the verb "to be," but the fabric of the rhizome is the conjunction, "and… and…and…." This conjunction carries enough force to shake and uproot the verb "to be" (Delueze & Guattari, 1994, 25).

The houses you see people having to live in are often appalling. They are broken down, smashed up. There is rubbish everywhere. The houses are hot—bloody hot—to live in. The air conditioner, if there is one, is most likely broken or not working because the electricity bill has not been paid. No one thought to insulate the house to make it stay cooler longer. The solar panels are smashed. The doors have been attacked by an axe. The windows are stuck together with cardboard and tape. Everything is wrong.

But you may have overlooked the small house nearby which is well kept and cool. The people in that house have jobs and can pay for the electricity for the air con; they can repair the door they have had to smash when they lose the key and can't get in so in desperation have taken to the door with an axe. (There is of course no locksmith for miles around and if there was one close by, it would be hours, days, weeks before they could manage to get to the job. And who can wait hours, days, weeks to have a feed, get cleaned up, have a nap?) The people in the small, well-kept house have time to clean up and chill out. They are probably not exactly healthy, because they have experienced the same terrible conditions as everyone else in the community, but they have somehow managed to scrape by and, because they have a bit of education, they can get something more than the dead end jobs—the "standing in a hole digging jobs," the "we don't want to do it but it is good enough for them" jobs—and so they can afford to go to the health center and get the drugs they need to manage their complex, often chronic, health issues. This house is probably filled to the brim with extended family because the extended family's house is smashed up and broken. And soon, because this house has so many people in it and the toilet, the laundry, the bathroom, the bedrooms are all overburdened, this house too will fail, and the family which has been doing so well until now will simply fall over under the stress of it; they will think "why do we bother?" and will let go the reins of the entire thing and fall apart too.

This situation can be found everywhere. I find it difficult to do housing in an Aboriginal community because I find it so infuriating. Each time I am approached to do some housing I say "no" and then I am talked into it. Each time after I have finally said "yes, I will do it" I imagine somehow, I will do things differently; that things will go differently. But they don't. And once again I wish I hadn't tried. Yet I know I will. Again. And again. And again.

What I Know About Aboriginal Housing

I know each room should be bigger than usual because they are likely to be occupied by a number of people—probably by more than the intended number.

I know the running costs of a house should be kept to a minimum because people have little disposable income and the cost of running and repairing a house can be crippling.

I know for costs to be minimized, the house should be environmentally sustainable. Most of the technology, however, is still new and not locally available so if it fails, it is expensive to repair and it can take a long time before someone gets there to repair it. People have been known to be without hot water for months because solar hot water or heat exchange systems have failed and there has been no one willing to go out to the community from the city and fix them. Besides, it is too expensive for just one to be repaired and it is better to wait until everyone else's hot water system fails too so they can all be fixed at once and make a bulk job of it.

I know plumbing, in particular, is a big issue and is always failing. This is in part because a lot of housing is on extremely reactive soil, which heaves and moves from water saturation or from drying out. Then, because the land around about is fairly flat, proper falls in sewerage and water pipes are difficult, and we all know shit flows downhill but if there is no downhill fall, or if the fall goes the other way back into the house, things turn ugly very quickly. This means the house should be off the ground some distance to insure sufficient falls in plumbing.

I know a lot of people will have mobility issues—either because of ill health or because they have small children in a pram. This means the house should be built directly on the ground.

I know together these two things contradict each other and a compromise has to be found.

I know people want to have a nice wide veranda to sit out on in the cooler part of the night—or to use as a sleep-out—or to have a meal on—but the funding never stretches this far—so the long western side of the house where the veranda should be is bald and the house becomes a hot box.

I know because of the way the streets have been laid out and because people want to have a front door facing onto the street, the orientation of the house can be tricky and this is another area of compromise.

I know the house people think they want and what might be best for the location, the orientation, the situation, are different and will never match up.

I know the space between the houses can be as important as the layout of the house itself and this is one area quickly forgotten as you move into the next phases of the house design.

I know none of this is what people want to hear about Aboriginal housing. They want to hear more interesting ideas as to different ways of living and how houses might reflect this. But first ask yourself: if you were always pointed out as "different" would you want yet another thing different about you? Do you feel confident enough to try out something entirely new?

Not likely. Most likely you would want your house and home to be the same as the everyday Australian House everyone else has—some improvements of course but pretty much the same.

What I Know About the Australian House

I know the Australian house is brick veneer—that is it has brick as an outside skin and a flimsy internal skin of studwork and plasterboard. If this type of house is not insulated properly, it is hot in summer and cold in winter and unless the internal studs are at close centers or you double up the plasterboard, it is easy to fall onto and make holes in.

I know the floor to ceiling height is likely to be 8' (240 cm) which makes it feel mean and boxlike inside; it will be difficult to install overhead ceiling fans or to add a good wide veranda, an element everyone yearns for, because too quickly, you run out of head room.

I know the house will look hot and tired in the blazing sun; the eaves around it will be narrow and mean, offering little protection from the sun or rain.

I know this house will look the same as all the others.

I know this house doesn't work the way it ought to, yet it is this house most people will want (or at least think they want)—a house the same as everyone else's, because surely not everyone can be so wrong.

WHAT I KNOW ABOUT CONSTRUCTION IN REMOTE AREAS

I know the materials and methods of construction should be sturdy so things won't fail quite so easily, because it can take so long before anything is fixed and in that length of time, other things will fail. It is best to make things fail-proof but this is almost impossible if you want a house to look like a house and not a prison.

I know it is best to make things out of locally available materials using locally available skills because of the difficulty of having things repaired if they get damaged or fail. At least if the things are available locally, they can be fixed comparatively quickly and cheaply.

I know the quality of workmanship is often poor, either because the non-Aboriginal tradesmen in town think it doesn't matter—or more cunningly think if it breaks down they will be called in to fix it and after all its government money so why shouldn't they get some of it—or it may be it is due to insufficient care or lack of training.

I know it is cheaper to pour a concrete slab-on-ground—or in places where there is highly reactive soil, a slab-on-a-mound—the mound being made up of imported fill which will erode and fall away and it will be difficult to get the pram up into the front door or to get uncle in his wheelchair into the house.

I know the construction of a house or houses within a community may be the most work the community members may get for some time and people like to have the opportunity to work on their own house and to gain some skills in the process if at all possible.

I know this employment and training of community members takes time and this will mean the house will be slower in construction and therefore it is easy to jump to the other side, to the other swing of the pendulum and have the houses transported in from a large town and locked into place on the site bringing more houses more quickly to a community but using less skills and therefore bringing less money into the community.

I know the construction of this housing gets caught into this cycle and it seems almost impossible to move on from these two means of delivery.

I know I am frustrated by it all, so what on earth can the community members be feeling and can any of this ever move along to be different?

I know one program, Housing for Health, takes small bite size pieces and fixes those things which can be fixed there and then. This program has collected copious statistics to prove that what is being done works. It employs local people, albeit in a small way, but it was eliminated in most Australian states by one line in a Government report.

I have read but can no longer find a story which goes something like this: An Aboriginal person in Central Australia was asked about their new house. "Yes," they said, "a house is a good thing. You can lock all your possessions in it and go away and leave them."

[P]eople have few personal belongings or assets, and in fact often only own a mattress, some blankets and a few clothes. Most often, people sleep in the yard, on the veranda, or in the main room of the house; the inside of the house is used for sleeping most often when it rains or when it is very cold. The interior of a typical Indigenous house at Yuendumu is mainly used for storage; many houses do not contain any furniture apart from some mattresses (Musharbash, 2001, 17).

This quote could be about any of the Aboriginal housing I have seen or been involved in.

House as a cupboard or storeroom. This is one solution, not only to Aboriginal housing, but to all housing. We need to move on from this idea of house and home as laden with aspiration. Aspiration can bring angst if the house does not deliver whatever it was that was wanted.

A house is a cupboard, nothing more, a place to lock things up and walk away from.

Warning! There is a danger in doing this translation work as there is danger in almost everything. You might find yourself thinking you understand more about a language than you actually do.

This danger of feeling confident in what you have done or could do is prevalent too in being overly confident in who you are.

WARNING WARNING

I have offered you what I know about the Australian house, about Aboriginal housing, about Aboriginal homes.

Following these exactly won't make the ideal
Australian house, the ideal Aboriginal house, the ideal
Aboriginal home. There are other things as important
perhaps more important.

The first is *listening*.

Listen to what you are being told. This listening
won't make you a great architect, not even a good
one. Most great architects, even good ones, know best.
They are steeped in ego. Most great architects, even
those considered good, are men. Men who make great
architects usually have enormous egos. They don't know
how to listen. And besides if they were to listen they
would know better than you anyway and it would have
been a waste of their time.

Listening will most probably have the client later
remark to a friend how "they" designed their house. It
will be only you who knows the part you played in this.

The second is *respect*.

If you respect and care for your clients a different
process occurs. I admire those who have a long (and
expensive) relationship with their clients—one they have
time to develop into a trusting relationship. I never had
the backing to be able to do this. I needed money to
live day to day. Perhaps it is still my problem. Perhaps
I should trust myself more. I never have. Instead I have
respect for my clients and trust they know best how they
want to live. Mostly I will do as I am asked, having first
explained the issues I can see in what they might want.
I have been known to say later to my partner I had told
them so. It is hard to hear back from a client—that such
and such doesn't work properly when you had already
told them and they had insisted.

I am still not certain how you get around this.

This hut…is like the shelter that some hunter might build for a night's lodging in the hills or like the cocoon some old silkworm might spin. (The Hojoki, 12)

Translating *Le*

In the quiet evenings I look out of my window -
the forest trees reach close up.
Behold the clusters of wisteria shining
like an allegory of our evil karma!

You yourself are a bird
clad in garments woven from wisteria vines
atop a hill convinced of the impermanence of all
earthly things
this fleeting evanescent nature of man

I see water and flowers offered to the Buddha
at a little basin I have made of piled up rocks
close by where I built a cottage just suited to my wants
I have abandoned the world and retired

This character is a kanji—English *le*; translation—
"house."

It was only much later I think to look up the Japanese
word for house and *le* comes up. I should have known.
Each time I stumbled on this hairy dragon, I wanted to
include le in my translations. It was telling me, but I kept
failing to listen to it, as I fail to listen to so many things.

GILLIAN BARLOW

I read that this kanji is made up of two characters—
one for roof, which makes sense, and the other for pig. I
could jump to the conclusion that it is more important
the family pig has somewhere to live than the humans
who look after the pig, but this seems too simple and I
don't know where or how I can find out more about this
idea.

Instead, I will take it at face value, as I see it—as a
hairy dragon.

Dragons symbolize wisdom, strength and hidden
knowledge. For many of us, our home is a place we seek
these. We hope to be wise and strong there, even if we
can't be like that out in the world. We need and want so
much from our house, yet it also brings with it the fire-
breathing properties of fear and attachment and so many
other things we don't need.

Although I tried to ignore *Ie*, it insisted on appearing
in my writing. I google "home" and come up also with *Ie*.
I finally make room for it.

I have written for ages on house and its alignment
with home, never quite resolving the issues I see. As an
architect, I build houses and hope they will become
"homes," yet I have no guidelines to ensure that they
do. Christopher Alexander's "A Pattern Language" has
patterns he and his team observed which he saw made a
place meaningful—that is, made a house a home. There
is no guarantee, however, that it works back the other
way—using the Alexander patterns does not guarantee
something will be homely.

I love my small train-like house. Each room is connected
to the next. It is not flash. It is only small but it is enough.
It needs a lot of repair work. If it is a dragon, it no longer

breathes fire as it ought. The roof leaks. The plaster ceiling is crumbling in one corner. The beams of the back porch are failing. The sliding doors keep jamming. It has few of Alexander's patterns. But I have lived here a long time now. It is in a location I love.

On the other hand, everything here is changing and I am no longer as convinced about that as I once was.

I sit typing in a small room with a low ceiling. I often stand up quickly, forgetting that it is so low. On the plus side, everything is within reach. The room is filled to brimming with books and small items meaningful only to me. I love writing here, trying to search out being at home with myself and who I am.

After a while I realise I don't mind much that I may be nothing special.

It suddenly occurs to me I ought to follow up on the Japanese word for home as well. If I were a solid logically systematic person no doubt I would have realized earlier that this was important.

I look up home in the translating site. It is surprising, but maybe not:

Le is house and home. It is household and housekeeping.

A gift.

BEING AT HOME

Many of us are not "at home" here, or anywhere. We are moved on, displaced, dispossessed, de-homed. We wave our arms and legs in front of us and look at them as though they are strangers, as though they belong to someone else. "Where are your feet?" people ask, and they look down, down, just as Alice did and there they are, right down there, miles away, not where you imagine them at all.

Where is your home, my home, our home? What do we mean by home?

Is the physical construction we live in our home?

Is home where we are from?

Or is there more to it?

How do we know this place of "home" or of "place"—a mix of language, roots, feeling of security, family and nostalgia?

I design houses for people and sometimes these become someone's home. Books are written about this. How a house becomes transformed into a home is a mystery.

I'm not sure I understand where my own home might be. It begins to get complicated as I continue to do this "home" work. Where is my home? How are home and place different or the same?

Aboriginal peoples speak of Country with a capital C—when does this change, if ever, to a lower-case country and what is the difference between the two? It feels like a similar discussion with house and home.

BALMAIN

I love the peninsula where I currently have my home despite its on-going gentrification by people who fail to stop and consider what living in a place that was once a strong working-class community might entail.

I have lived around this peninsula since I first moved to this big city. As a student, my first house in the area was a ramshackle four bedroom with flimsy canvas paintings tacked to the ceiling, door frames and floor to form walls.

The bathroom was under the house where it was damp and mouldy. There was a large red bath. A bath had been one of our must-have criteria for renting. But this was a bathroom for which we once called in the Local Government Health Inspector. The landlord had refused to fix the toilet which kept overflowing. We wanted our rent re-credited. The Health Inspector arrived in his long white socks and shorts, clutching his clipboard. As he told us, everything seemed okay to him (we were, after all, only renting), he flicked his cigarette butt into the toilet. We were shocked—not that he continued smoking in our house and then threw the butt into the toilet but he hadn't flushed it after doing so! End of story.

The house had views across the city which included the iconic Sydney Harbour Bridge. There was a jungle-y garden with feijoa trees, mangoes and a million mosquitoes. When I finally managed to hack my way with a machete down to the back fence, I found wire sculptures and a fire pit.

The neighbor, Shirley, would spy on us from her house on the higher side of the hill. She had lived in the neighborhood her whole life. The place had once been filled with wharfies and dockies. It was a very working-class place beginning to be overtaken by artists and writers, and now students like ourselves. After a few months, Shirley decided we weren't too bad. We didn't make as much noise as others in the neighborhood had told her we would. She took to making us choko chutney and having long chats with us through the gaps in the paling fence.

I love the whole peninsula with its tight steep streets and small "dunny" (privy) lanes, which once provided access to the dunny so the nightsoil man could come to empty it and now meant secret passages criss-crossed the suburb.

I have lived here for decades. Who cared if there were power stations on either side of the peninsular so black soot had to be wiped off the windscreen when you got up in the morning and you had to rewash your washing if you left it for too long on the clothesline? I have lived in houses all over these hilly extents—sometimes by the water, often with broad city views, mostly on the slopes of its high spine surrounded by other workers cottages. When I was forced by rising rents to move off the peninsula ("Make sure you take your passport!" people joked) I had to return there to get my bearings in order to drive to any other place.

I'm not sure I feel it is my home, though. While I would not want to live anywhere else in this city, I've never felt as though I belong in this city. When I first moved here as a student, I was neither working class nor an artist. Now that it has been gentrified, I don't feel I belong amongst the bankers and insurance managers. But I love this place surrounded by harbor.

BETHANY

Home could be Bethany.

I love going to Bethany although it is not a place where I have ever lived. It is a small village outside of Tanunda on the edge of the Barossa Valley, one of the major wine making areas of South Australia. There are five houses. On every trip to Adelaide no matter what the reason, we drive out to visit.

My mother grew up in Tanunda. I have never lived there either, nor anywhere very close to either of these places. It is "home" regardless. It is a place of certainty and knowing, my mother's homeland.

My father must have felt overwhelmed by all of this "mother's family's home" stuff. Although he enjoyed going to Tanunda. At least it could provide those things he felt a home should provide—fine food and wine.

Whenever we visited my grandmother in Adelaide during the hellish heat of December, a trip to Tanunda would be suggested and then, with much enthusiasm, the trip would be organized as though we had never been there before. Year after year we would make this same trip to Tanunda, travelling much the same route, seeing much the same things, buying much the same food and drinks from much the same shops. Variations would be suggested, and at times even included, but they were always slightly disappointing and although nothing would be said, they would not be included on future trips and we would revert to our favorites.

There we are—we grandchildren in the Chevy with my grandfather, my grandmother and my father. The Chevy has more legroom than the other car, so my father accompanies us, although it is hoped he would prefer to travel with my uncle since they have both have "manhood" in common. My father, however, is not one for fixing things or knowledgeable about cars or any other type of mechanical things or aeroplanes or…. He doesn't read the Wilbur Smith books my uncle loves. No, he hides behind more theoretical texts, preferring books on stamps and jazz.

My grandfather's hat sits stolidly on the back shelf, warning those who can read such signs to stay clear, here is a hat-driver.

In the other vehicle are our mother, our aunty and uncle and their two children, our cousins.

My grandfather's car always leads the expedition. My grandfather excitedly points out familiar things, slapping the steering wheel hard with his left arm and then, leaning across my grandmother, follows the direction of his arm with his head, his eyes no longer watching the road. He points with his right arm towards her side window. "There!" He glances into the rearview mirror to make sure that we—my father, my brothers and I—are looking where he is pointing. "There!" he says again, triumphantly, emphasizing a point he has made several times on this trip as part of his running commentary on "going to Tanunda." It might be to point out the Heidiflour Salisbury Mill which my mother's family is, or was, associated with, or where my father used to work when we still lived in Adelaide, or perhaps the turn off to my friend Annabel's farm on One Tree Hill.

He then will start the discussion with my grandmother as to the order of things—should we go via Bethany and visit the cemetery and then head on to Schlinky's Gully for the picnic, or go straight into Tanunda via great-grandmother's house and get the mett first up? This is code for: do we have enough food for a picnic or will we need mettwurst and bread and sharm cakes as well?

Whatever the order, at some stage of this trip, we will drive past great-grandmother's house.

"There!" someone will say.

The car slows down. The car has no air conditioning. It is summer and it is so hot the windows have to be wound right down, although it would be better if they were up because the hot dry air blows in and around the car, making it hotter and dryer inside. And with the windows down, the number of flies inside increases and they buzz ceaselessly around our faces.

Our heads turn as one to look.

"There!" the someone says again. The car slows. It is almost stopping. The dazzling heat blasts us. We all look.

We drive past. It is a house with a central solid timber door and a double-hung window on either side—like a children's drawing of a house. There is a change of pitch in the roof to form a deep veranda at the front. There are few distinguishing features.

Time slows momentarily and then speeds up again and we are past.

That's it.

Grandfather stamps his foot onto the accelerator, the car surges forward and our heads are thrown back with the thrust.

That is all we see of great grandmother's house. But it is an introduction to the stories of a childhood growing up in a German village away from Germany, of a life spent constantly roaming from one relative's house to the next, of dead bodies lying in state in the front room so it is best to enter a house via the back door just in case— this for those of us present who have never experienced it.

Food, or fear of the lack of it, is a driving force. We will need to buy the mettwurst and the fritz for the picnic from the same deli where great grandma bought it—it would be sacrilege to buy it from anywhere else even if it is better there.

Going inside, we have much the same conversation as though we had been coming in each day for the past thirty years.

"Hello there. Good to see you. How are the grand children?"

"Have you seen what they have done to the old house? Oooh, is that right?"

"You'll have the mett then. With or without the garlic?"

"They're good and soft. You know there is always someone who wants the hard ones though."

"Would the kiddies like a slice of the fritz? Thick or thin? How many were you after?"

"They never make enough sharm cakes, do they? Look at that! We're almost out already. Ooh, there could be enough though. Lucky you! Would you like them all? Shall I pack them in a box or are you eating them now? We'll have more next time you're in—they're making them now."

The car gradually becomes awash with the strong meaty smells of salamis and fritzs.

We drive to our picnic spot near Bethany via the cemetery where we drop in to visit the family. We walk through the headstones, pausing and reading each one off as though we have never seen them before, and must question who each was and work out their role. Finally, we arrive at the picnic shed at Schlinky's Gully. This is the heart of the visit. We lay out the food on the table and slump into place.

The heat is awful. The heat is unbearable. It is so hot that eating seems like the last thing you'd do. We pretend for a bit that we might be tempted to hoe into the enormous spread set out before us, but we all know what is coming next. We sit stiffly in our knowing, dreading the request.

"How about a fire?" my grandmother finally suggests enthusiastically.

It is a rhetorical question. We file out of the picnic shed, which has been holding the heat firmly down on our heads and walk slap bang into the horizontal heat from the sun. Stunned, we begin the search for twigs and sticks.

My grandma will build an almighty fire. She'll watch for a bit whilst one or other of us has a go at doing it, tutting to herself, pointing at various sticks or bits of log which need to be moved slightly or taken out. Finally, she'll be forced to come over and rescue it and within minutes it will roar into life.

She will then sit happily for the rest of the afternoon poking a stick at it, poking logs or sticks ever so slightly, commanding someone to go and fetch a bit more fuel for the fire—a stick yay long by this thick. She will hold up her rickety finger and measure one against the other to indicate how thick a stick she would like—commenting over and over about what a good fire it is, reminiscing of the other fires she has had here. My grandma, happy, sitting stoking the fire until well after dark.

And then it is time to drive back to Adelaide again.

The same thing. It is always the same thing. That's what home is—a place where everything is the same, where things are always familiar, always as they were. If something changes even ever so slightly, it is immediately apparent and the resulting gossip rages through the streets like a bushfire with cries from all directions of "Change Back! Change Back! Change back!"

RED DIRT

I love red dirt country—not any particular "red country" place but all red country. It draws me in. I become a different me in red dirt country. I feel it in my bones, in my heart, as I drive out from a town or city.

As I leave the city, there is nothing but driving, only driving, me and the bitumen, me and the movement of the car through landscape, me and...then I hit the red dirt.

It leaps up and grabs me, wrestles me by the neck to get me to pay attention and then gradually seeps into my very depths.

The air smells different. The earth smells different. There is the smell of salt bush I love. Suddenly there are eagles. Sometimes they are on the side of the road sitting atop a carcass of roadkill. Sometimes they are circling overhead. There is stillness. I am sure people who live here don't notice this silence, they are so used to it.

How would I be if I lived out here? Would I slow to a halt or would I become something, someone else?

Red dirt moves me into my body, like the sensation I feel as I begin to write, my whole body involved; or sometimes when I do aikido—when sometimes I forget "me" and become engaged in this flow.

This is me in red dirt, a gathering together, a moving through rather than a falling apart.

Surely this is home.

...we should shun all clinging to the world of phenomena, so that the affection I have for this thatched hut is in some sort of sin. (The Hojoki, 20)

Translating *To* and *Te*

と

Like a drifting cloud,
he is a person of little account
his feelings are like those of
a sparrow near a hawk's nest

Spring and summer were scorching hot
the hills crumbled then roared up in flames —
some deserted their land
some wondered at such a sight

I listen to the rustle of the maples
I am in the mood for music
I can make a fire of broken brushwood
but have little skill in music or verse

This character, と, is a hiragana—English text *to*;
translation—"when."

て

A garden surrounded by a thin low brushwood fence
I contemplate the scenery and meditate
all alone.

This character, て, is a hiragana—English text *te*; translation—"hand."

I used the Haiku structure to write the poems for both *to* and *te*.

Hand it to me
to choose *to*
when I start!

I chose と and then included て because of how they appeared to a non-speaking, non-reading, non-writing, non-Japanese person. They seemed to represent my attitude towards this project of translation.

Both looked to me to be a person about to spring into action, bending eagerly towards that which will follow, tossing away anything that might tie it down, eager to launch into life.

と, *to*, swings its arms high up behind itself not sure whether it will leap up or forward. Its body is a spring, keen for the leap but unclear as to where it is aiming or where it might land.

て, *te*, is more controlled. It also has its arms swung back but they are more directed. It is about to dive into a pool, head tucked, ready to race. It is clear this character understands that if it is to get to the end of the pool first, or even get there at all, it is necessary to dive far over the water, have the goal clearly in mind, and then swim for its life. It knows too the importance of form and style. It is driving onward to completion.

I first chose the less directed character, と, over て. Should I read into this that I did not know where I was aiming? That I did not know where I would land? Or why or even if I would land at all?

116

As I went through the text and replaced to with the selected image, *to* became confused with *te*. When placed side by side, it is easy to see the differences. But staring at the text with its many unknown characters, it is easier to understand how I could not tell them apart. The two hiragana sit together, *to* is *Ready*, and *te* is *Set*.

I wait for the Go!

Go! which as luck might have it can be the same in Japanese.

Go?

I stood for a long time at the end of a pool waiting for the right moment—waiting for that Go! But no starter gun sounded. I would have to set off on my own.

I had written and rewritten so many times my exegesis, my drafts, my book. I stood and stood, hesitating and hesitating.

I wanted the Hojoki to be used as many use the Bible—for bibliomancy, as an oracle. And for myself as well—in each translation I hoped I would find something different.

When I started, the kanji were unfamiliar to me. I slowly picked my way through the text and gradually began to be able to identify and separate them. As I spent more and more time with the Japanese text, I became increasingly familiar with them. I noticed subtle differences I had failed to see before—just as the colonialists failed to see the differences in the Country they invaded. They failed to see, to seek, to know any differences among the Aboriginal Nations. Yet now, perhaps, they too can begin to see more.

When I first began translating by inserting housing photos into a text, I failed to recognize this also was a colonizing project.

I did these substitutions to see if the text would reveal something different to me. In the end it has, but not what I expected. I wanted it to reveal something to me about space, place, time, housing—and more, something about me—but it has revealed to me how difficult it is to do this.

My first translation was hard to do. As I substituted more and more tiny photos, they shrank to a size where they became indistinguishable from each other and took more and more memory of the computer. To print a single page on my home printer took up to a half an hour. A commercial printer was much faster but produced faint ill-defined replicas of what I wanted. My home printer did better reproductions, so I was printing any pages with colored photos slowly at home and inserting them later into the manuscript. This slowness became a limiting factor. I saw that I would never be able to substitute all the characters in the text. My computer would never have enough memory to do so. I was unable to find any apps to assist me with this.

I worked to the very limit of what my computer could do. Then I stopped.

But what really halted me in my writing was my search for certainty.

I have looked everywhere for certainty, and to know what being certain might mean to me. I want to be certain about who I am. I want to be authentic. I want to be wholly me. Even if I name the things I am sure of, I am always left with a residual doubt. I never feel as though they quite fit.

I am not certain I am an architect. Although I completed six years of an architectural degree, sat the exams and been successful as a registered architect, I don't feel like one. The architectural skills I have are no long required; I cannot do computer aided drafting. It is unlikely I could get a job in an architectural office any longer.

I never felt I was one of the architectural students gang who were extremely certain as to what they were doing and how it should be done. I hung out with them; tried wearing this certainty as a coat, but it dragged on the ground: the arms were too long. Their comments never sat true in me.

I was told what was good architecture but when I got inside the building, it didn't always hum. I know I am supposed to like the Sydney Opera House, for example, and while I kind of do, I rarely go there or hang out there to be in its aura.

So I have never been certain that I would know a good place if I were to stumble upon it.

But hang on, that isn't right!

Last year in Barcelona, a place I had been decades before and had not been to since, I visited all the Gaudi buildings I could—Casa Mila, Casa Battlo, Sagrada Familia, Parc Guel, and fell in love with them all over again. So many things I thought could not possibly work were there! They restored my belief in architecture.

I would never be able to do such things—never could be so experimental or bold or have such an intuitive sense of how things ought to be. As an architect, I am too timid,

119

too concerned with what the client wants. I could never tell someone, the person paying me for example, that my idea is better than theirs. And in Australia there are so many rules and regulations that there is no possibility of doing as Gaudi did. But I spent every minute of every day in Barcelona in a Gaudi building. They are amazing.

And of course, Le Corbusier, another architect who had absolute certainty about his ability and vision. He also made great places to be in. He is often thought of as a cold, egotistical man. But I have visited a few of his buildings that are inspiring. His Ronchamp Chapel is how a building for worship should be. One enters it and falls into awe.

I am uncertain, too, about my belief as a Buddhist. I question too much, but I don't question the teacher. I sit in meditation each morning but I can't say I understand what it is I am doing or if I am doing it correctly or if I have progressed. I am not even sure what progression might be.

Even if I were to come to some sense of certainty, I realize I would never be absolutely certain. Because if someone were to question me, I would hesitate and listen to their truth and then go back and question mine.

For example, I wanted to disown my great great great Grandfather and his missionary life. He was not only a missionary but German as well. This part of my heritage I felt I need not inhabit. But as I explored his life, I began to think maybe he had not been all bad and he may even have done some good. I watched the film The Songkeepers and could appreciate that the missionaries translating Lutheran hymns into Aranda which were then taken back to Germany a century later to sing was a "good" thing. By doing these early translations, the Aranda language has been preserved—Aboriginal people were mostly forbidden to talk in language during early colonization; without language it was of course much more difficult to maintain culture. Even now, there continues to be a reluctance for schooling to be done in language or for it to be taught.

I have spent a lot of time in my career making guidelines for Aboriginal housing so people can deliver with some certainty what the guidelines indicate. I began this work with enthusiasm, certain I had something to contribute. In the first guidelines, I wrote everything I knew about how to do Aboriginal housing and explained the reasons. I assumed a project manager was interested in the reasons why something was done, but discovered that in fact they were not. They wanted to only do those things they needed to do so they could do the job "right" and collect their money.

In subsequent guidelines I didn't make the same mistake. They were much vaguer. With the guidelines for disability housing, they needed to be deliberately loose. Everyone was an individual and needed their own written guidelines—uncertainty was built into these. Do this if…but you may need to do something very different depending….

Most people don't want to go away from a film or a book with a sense of uncertainty. They want to know the ending, and tiptoeing around or leaving an open ending does not make them happy. Most people want to go away feeling certain about a book or film—or life. Certain they know how things end. Certain everything will be all right. Certain the time they spent reading was well spent.

But what if there isn't any certainty, and the sense of certainty is a myth?

From dabbling in Buddhism, I know the only thing that doesn't change is change itself. As soon as you find something to grasp hold of, it disappears and appears somewhere else. Over there. Now here. Back there.

I am not certain about who I am. And yet this is what I am exploring here, in the hope by the end of this exercise I will be certain.

Most fiction works this way moving from a place of less to more certainty so the reader can talk about the journey they have been on.

What would make me feel certain? Is there such as a thing as being totally certain?

If I google "certainty," I find there are centuries of searching for the meaning of certainty. There is "I think, therefore I am" but I am not even sure I think, so therefore maybe I am not. And maybe the uncertainty will always be there regardless. This is perhaps why we need religions and everything else we have constructed, so we feel certain? We want to know we will continue and since we will never know this, we make other certainties. Even a Ouija board never tells us exactly what we hope for.

At my center, therefore, there is an uncertainty. I am not certain. Well, I am certain of this uncertainty so perhaps I am certain after all.

I sat on the edges of town, a place where those excluded from the life of the town lived, those who had addiction and mental health issues and where they had been pushed to, a place surrounded by scrubby bush, broken houses, dirt and sky, a place quietly beautiful and heard my friend say to those around her, "Ask her surname."

No-one did as though they were afraid to.

Perhaps they hadn't heard her say it.

She was certain about me, certain she knew things about me. My surname meant something to her and the others there, something I didn't understand at the time, something that might connect me to that place. The history of Australia and its colonization, the massacres that occurred everywhere across the lands, are still not talked about. I worried at her knowing my surname and its connection to that place.

On my return to the city, this stayed with me and I wondered why she might have asked. The place lingers with me longer than most places do. Then I had no reason to connect myself to it. That is changing. I was not clear then why this might have happened—I am clearer now. More certain at least but still caught in my habit of never being totally certain, of never saying a definite "yes" or "no" but the in-betweens—maybe, perhaps, I guess.

I was humble as I accepted my friend's comment. I didn't ask her what she meant. My "feelings (were) like those of a sparrow near to a hawk's nest" (The Hojoki, 11) — certain in my trust that she knew what she was saying, uncertain as to where it might lead our friendship.

I wonder at certainty.

We all know how miserably certainty can pan out, particularly if we know about Bertrand Russell's Inductivist Turkey. We are living proof of it. Each morning we see ourselves getting up and going about the world. Each day is much the same. Each day we assume we will do it again on the morrow. Until the day the virus strikes and we can no longer go outside.

> I have always been uncertain.
> Maybe that is what I like.
> That is the edge I play.
> I am an uncertain Buddhist.
> I am an uncertain architect.
> I am an uncertain writer.
> I am an uncertain poet.
> I am uncertain in who I am.

Maybe everyone is uncertain. I think of those bombastic people who always appear certain. I have worked with some of these. They didn't know as much as they thought they did. Their lack of knowledge made no difference to them. They ran the project into the ground, refusing to listen to anyone else.

Maybe being certain isn't all it is cracked up to be.

NOMADOLOGY

It mostly starts with driving.

It starts with driving hesitantly.

I remember I wanted to explore movement in writing and in space, how movement, time and space might locate place—not driving.

This was some type of *ma*, something I had been fascinated about for some time.

I knew I wanted to explore nomadology further, with its seeming relationship to *ma*.

I know I want to drive with more certainty.

What is nomadology?

The word appears in one of my favorite books, *Reading the Country: Introduction to Nomadology*.

Nomadology comes from Deleuze and Guattari, French philosophers who wrote A *Thousand Plateaus*, a book I tried reading but which quickly became impenetrable. In a good way, though.

It is extraordinarily satisfying to read this type of philosophical text. From it, images and ideas quickly spring up. It is because the ideas are so wild and unfathomable that your brain has a chance to place different thoughts together and make something else entirely from them. You may have understood something correctly. Or you may not have. Most likely you haven't understood a word but that is okay because something else has been sparked.

The concept of nomadology appealed to me in the first instance because of the word "nomad" and all this word conjures, rightly or wrongly. Since first visiting the Atlas Mountains, I have thrilled to the thought of "nomads." It is not really how we imagine it, particularly in Australia. It was always paired with words such as camels or tents, always crossing mountains. I don't think I even connected the word to Australia. Despite what we were taught at school, Aboriginal Australians are not nomadic, they are at the most semi-nomadic.

Nomadism varies from nation to nation. It seems to me nomad was a propaganda term used to justify the colonizers stealing Country in order to own it. If people moved broadly around anywhere and anyway they chose, then it wouldn't matter if someone, a white colonialist squatter for example, took that land. If you consider Country as a large estate—which is what it was before colonization—it makes sense that you would need to travel constantly over and around it to make sure everything was running smoothly.

I am a different type of nomad. The jobs I love involve driving across the country, stopping to engage with a community, to spend a night gazing at the sky, to get up in the morning—in winter to restart the fire and clutch my cup of brewed coffee in hands tucked into the end of my jumper's sleeves and watch the steam come from my mouth or to walk slowly before dawn to the edges of town and back—in summer-time hoping I might at last use the pastels and paper I carry with me to draw the country's beauty at dawn. Regardless of whether I travel alone or with others, I always make time to be by myself in country.

If one has no wings he cannot fly, and unless one is
a Dragon, he will find it difficult to ride the clouds.
(The Hojoki, 9.)

BOUNDARY CROSSING

DRIVING

I LOVE DRIVING. When I was young, my family would drive from Canberra to Adelaide then a two day drive- for Christmas. It doesn't seem as far anymore, but in our old Mercedes, or later my father's flash new Fiat 124 Sports car, it took much longer.

The Mercedes had plenty of room to move in. It was old, though, heavy and not built for speed. The new Fiat travelled fast but was small—even smaller once you squashed two adults in the front, three children, a dog and the luggage in the back. Perhaps it taught me to be still, to ponder the external and internal worlds.

The road to Adelaide through the Hay Plain is long, straight, and flat, and travelling at Christmas meant it was also hot. Little varies outside on either side of the car for mile after mile. I would enter a dozing world. Speech was rare. For the two days it took us, we were in a time capsule, our daily needs set to "simple," with food three times a day, sleep at its end and little else.

We would squabble about who sat in the middle, who was allowed to pass out the snacks, who was leaning on whom and was this permissible. But we knew to keep these conversations low, or risk being in trouble.

Driving with my family was a dreaming involving the never-ending road, sky, a landscape continuing on either side of the car seemingly forever. When the car finally stopped, my parents would get out of the front of the car, and we would get out from the back, bowing our heads as though we were about to fall, or perhaps as though on bended knees being presented to the Dalai Lama.

The first steps of release were a stagger. The white heat nearly blacked you out. There might be something to eat and drink at as this place, we would think, a pub with no ice or with its dining room just this minute closing. It was a lesson in acceptance, flexibility and patience. Mindfulness too, as you gathered up the items you may need from the car.

The time spent out of the car became less significant than the time spent inside it. The continuous sound of the car's engine and the wheels across the bitumen surface, are like a medieval drone, or a mantra. I watched out across the flat land wondering why there were no trees, why trees were only along rivers, whether there were there trees before and what had happened to them. If I leaned back, I could look out the sloping back window which focused the sunshine onto our heads, and watch the clouds and sky. It was a time of hyperspace and cocooning—a hibernation of sorts. Perhaps a re-generation.

Whenever I go on a long drive I drift readily into a dreaming state.

On long drives I began to understand place viscerally. The places along the drive were linked by long stretches in which nothing much seemed to be occurring except imagining and humming to yourself in the car, inventing stories or dreaming. We were astronauts zooming through landscape in a semi-woken state, only without their exotic space foods or floating around the spaceship or chance of bouncing out with a flag and stating "One step...."

Sometimes we would be encouraged to make up songs or tell stories or play eye-spy but mainly we sat in silence, bearing the heat in a car with no air conditioning or radio. One of us might suddenly burst into our most favorite driving song, one we had written ourselves many years before, Around the corner and under the trees... and then fall silent again. Or everyone might join in and we would invent a few more verses.

As a result now we are older we can sit amiably in silence for long lengths of time and not expect much to happen.

Travelling with other people not-related isn't always so amiable, especially after hours and hours of sitting in an enclosed box. Assumptions are made. Most cars now have stereos and air conditioning, which make things both easier and more difficult. Who dictates what is listened to, how loudly and for how long? Who controls the temperature of the car? Is fresh air better than the car's recycled air?

Sometimes I drive in the work car with others and we chat about this and that. Sometimes we sit quietly together with only the noise of tires of the car on the road. Sometimes we have the radio on, listening to music or some fool chatting as if we might be interested in their opinion. Sometimes, and I like this best, I gaze out of the window of the moving car and wonder, allowing the road and landscape and sky to drift through me at its own pace.

We decide to go for a drive, failing to obtain the necessary permissions from anyone, moving with the arrogance of city folk. Driving gives us a sense of purpose. After another hour or so on a dirt road, we stop, get out of the car and walk around to stretch our legs. No one speaks. There is nothing to comment on. There seems to be nothing here, although if we could see properly we would find all sorts of things of interest. We stand and peer at the sun beginning to set in the huge sky. Then we get back into the car and turn it around for "home." The fear of hitting a kangaroo or an emu, for now it is the hour when they are moving, means driving more slowly. Long plumes of dust no longer follow the car as they had on the drive out. We drive fearfully, trying to anticipate the animals' movements, unused to the shifting surface of the fine red dirt road.

Sometimes at the end of the day if there is a gap in time before the next appointment, someone might suggest we go for a bit of a drive. We hop in the car together again. With my work companions, we can drive in any direction and be no closer and no farther from anywhere else.

On these evening trips, it is usually Keith who drives. He handles the car well on the feet-thick red sand. We travel so fast we don't see or feel the ridges like sea waves in the road. We hit things at times although we don't see them, as they haven't seen us. They bump off the car. Ridges. Emus. Bug-eyes. Locusts. Verges. Roos.

We may arrive at a somewhere—a place of local note, a place we know the name of. We may not. Eventually we turn back, stopping first to get out of the car. Keith walks to the passenger seat. I get into the driver's seat.

I always drive back.

"I'll keep a watch out for roos," Keith says and folds his arms over his chest and goes to sleep.

I drive without the same desperate speed as Keith. I drive with a desperate need not to hit anything. It takes four to five times longer to return than it took to get there.

How would it be to know country so well you could travel anywhere and know exactly where it was you were at any moment, certain you know how to move on and where you will end.

Katy is driving.

Keith is sitting in the back.

I am sitting in the front next to Katy.

A disco tape is playing, one Keith had insisted we put on. It is impossible to hear clearly over the sound of the wheels on the road, the air whipping past the windows. It has a good strong beat though—regular, like the kilometer markers. The cassette clicks and turns to play the other side, over and over, backwards and forwards, uninterrupted in a continuous unheard stream just like those kilometer markers.

"Turn it up!" Keith shouts from the back after a length of time.

Neither Katy nor I move.

There is no malice or misunderstanding. Keith wants this tape. Neither Katy nor I minds though we are not in the mood for music. But to do as we are told would have extracted too much energy.

We are certain we will get there eventually.

The interior atmosphere of the car stretches in all directions and flattens out.

I feel it in the pit of my stomach, as if a stone has fallen there and landed with a thud. The flatness is apparent once the ripples of the stone reach my stomach's walls and sink there.

The sky is a cliché dome above. Its springing points at the horizon on either side are barely visible even though there is no tree or bush or cloud to hinder the sight of it. It is so far away. The huge orb of sky encases and gently balances us in its center for its own purposes.

The silence stretches like a rubber band between us. Me here. You there. We sit and drive. A bump is all it would take for it to snap back to slack.

The exterior landscape drifts by forever and ever.

I'm certain I've been here before, the flat terrain continues to feel familiar.

I am certain there has been a conversation between us and we understand each other better as a result of this silent driving.

I'm driving. It's raining. The windscreen wipers beat. The rain tapping on the car roof is reminiscent of the way it sounds on a tin veranda roof. The rain forms rivulets in the earth. Small rivers depositing water to seeds. These begin germinating almost as we drive past. Small blades of green peeping out of the shiny red earth. Water pools at the edge of the road. Papers, plastic cups, sticks, skeletons, tissues spiral slowly along in the developing rivers.

The colors of county are polished up, the red made redder, the brown, the beige. Dead green slowly ripens to alive green again. Rivulets cut into the earth showing its history.

The smell of dirt, foliage, rain is intense. You know it will rain well before it starts, because of the smell. Then comes the blackening sky. The instant you are certain, the rain is upon you.

I am driving with the window down. Droplets of rain blow off the wind protector onto my arm. It's surprisingly cold. The inside of the car is beginning to cool.

"Wind the fuckin' window up ya mongrel, woodja?" Keith shouts.

I hesitate a moment before reluctantly doing as I am told.

The rain gets harder.

I turn the wipers up a notch. I change the tune running inside my head to match the faster beat of the wipers.

"The wheels on the bus go round and round, round and round, round and round...." Why is it always some annoying song you had forgotten you remembered, all those rainy kilometers?

I am certain this is how it happened although I am not so sure of the details.

Don't worry, I know where I am headed. I'll stop when I get there.

Whirring across the country. Up mountains. Through ever thinning forests. Past the one-tree hills. Down onto the open plains. Along the bitumen. Through the dirt.

135

Even with my eyes shut, I know.

Here. I say and I open my eyes.

The very last of the brown, black, sandy soil is past.

Here.

And we are into the red.

I change with the color of dirt.

I know myself here. I feel certain and proud. I love it here in the red dirt.

Yes, it's hot but it's a dry heat not a humid heat and as long as I move comparatively slowly I'll be fine. I'll skulk around the edges of things—buildings, trees—to remain in the shade where it is cooler. I know this. I always look for shady places to park the car. Even if it means I have to walk a bit further. As long as you walk slowly, don't rush, dry heat is fine.

DIRT DREAMS

My clearest memory is one I have always had from the beginning.

There are two rocking chairs. A large one and a miniature one. I sit in the miniature one rocking.

There is a large woman in the other rocking chair. Her hair is curly and black and is swept back and tied in a red kerchief. She smiles down at me. She leans out over her large round bosom to show me what it is she is making. She is embroidering a hankie. Her black hands hold it out towards me, to explain to me its meaning. She tells me that she is making it for me.

I hold my small hands out to touch the colored threads she is using. She takes my hands in hers. The only difference is the size. I marvel at the similarities. Big hand. Little hand. Both are dark. I rock backwards and forwards. With her. We are sisters.

Later I ask my mother about this memory, one of only a few I have of my childhood.

"Tell me!" she says.

I begin to describe what I see.

"Why would you remember that!" my mother says. "Could be."

As a child, I would tear my clothes off and cover myself in dirt. Squatting in front of a small pile of sticks and leaves, I would remove two flints from a stained embroidered hankie. I would place them gently beside me. I would hold the hankie, and let it flap in the breeze. I would examine its edges, caress the stitches, which were slowly undoing themselves and then smooth it out on the ground in front of me. I would place the flints in its center. Words formed in my mind and I would slowly, slowly hum them, each time getting louder, more certain.

After some time, I would pick up the flints and strike them.

Over and over.

Always humming.

I would keep striking the flints, until there was a wisp of smoke. I would fan the flame with an exercise book from which pages had been torn to feed the fire. When the fire was burning confidently and could fend for itself, I would go and remove from a hollow in a tree, two sticks and clap them together. I would begin to sing more loudly still, the words appearing before me as a vision. In the trees, the birds were suspended, hypnotized as I sang.

My best friend was involved too.

I would talk to her quietly to convince her. She was always scared at first. She would look nervously towards the window where her mother might be standing, hands in a sink of lemon-scented detergent. Her mother had warned her not to listen to me. I would continue quietly. I would tell her stories of ants eating people—*alive.* Ghosts who would bury people—*still struggling.* Of girls just like her, whose thick blonde healthy hair fell out in sheaves, dark splotches appearing over their bodies, eyes *gradually becoming blind.*

She had no choice. She was under my spell.

On this day, I sit down to go through my drawings and notes. For a moment I close my eyes. I am exhausted. When I open them again, there is someone in front of me.

She is large and black. She has on a yellow gingham frock. A red kerchief ties back her hair. Her feet have calloused soles from walking long distances in bare feet. She stands swaying, a flagon of cheap sherry in one hand. Eyes turned inwards, she grins at me. She knows I am watching.

She speaks softly at first and is barely audible. I strain to hear. Her talking gets louder. She starts cursing, then she is yelling at me. Or it could be at herself. Or at the world. She goes on and on, cursing and swearing at me, at the world, at herself.

"Garn ya mug," she yells, swinging the flagon. I duck and weave to avoid being struck. But I tire soon and decide to take the punches, the slurs instead. These seem to strengthen me.

I wonder who she might be. I am reminded of a woman I met in a shopping mall in Central Australia while travelling. She had stopped me very deliberately and handed me a necklace made of local seeds and pods. I had been touched. I felt chosen. I immediately put the necklace around my neck.

After the requisite day at home to recover from the trip, I go back to work. I swagger into the office with a bravado I have not had before. This is not the meek, mild-mannered me. This is someone else entirely. If I don't agree with something, I say, "Fuck off you arse hole, you're talking crap!"

It shocks people and I enjoy this. Everyone moves their desks away from mine, at first only a bit and then further and further. This gives me space and power. My workmates re-arrange their workstations so that they are facing away from me. They make sure they sit as far from me as possible. It's great. At last I have enough room to be able to talk on the phone without feeling that everyone is leaning in, listening to me. I can fling my arms around and gesticulate wildly, as though I have a flagon in my hand. I can spread all my documents, books, pens, pencils and get a good look at them.

At one point, I notice out of the corner of my eye, that the boss is coming towards me. I can guess what he's about to say, "Everyone is complaining about you and your behavior." I look up and glare at him. He swerves suddenly as though he never intended to come my way at all. I smile first to myself and then laugh loudly so everyone can hear.

Soon the woman in the gingham yellow frock starts to be around all the time, behind me, egging me on, always in the periphery of my vision. If I turn to face her, she has gone but I know she's still there on the edges. The level in the flagon is decreasing. She's getting drunker and drunker. I am getting louder and more raucous at the same rate. I am egged on by her comments from behind her hand. Her nod and "go on," pushing me forward. Ever braver, I say what I've always wanted to say. I'm going places! People daren't stop me or get in my way. Each day I look forward to getting to work to see what's going to happen, to see whom I run into and can shock.

A few days later, however, something changes again. I am not "me" anymore. I seem to have forgotten how to look after myself. I am not eating. I don't feel hungry, only thirsty. I swig down large volumes of water to quench an ever-worsening dehydration. I use a large glass flask and carry it around with me instead of a cup. I appear thin—not so much physically but it's as though you can see through me. I'm tired. It is like being sick without being sick. At the end of the work-day, I stagger home and drop in front of the TV. I stare at the flickering screen uncomprehendingly. Perhaps I'm a soapie character. My thoughts are broken into seven-minute time bites. Nothing is resolved. Every strand is left to hang. Too soon all thoughts fade to a pinpoint at the center of my mind. I am a blank screen. I fall asleep.

I am required to do a site visit. My companions, Katy and Keith are mysteriously busy and say they can't come even though mainly they will jump at any chance to get out of the office. I head off by myself. I am in the car driving when with a start, I wonder what I am doing. Where am I? How did I get here? I know I am meant to be somewhere but am unclear as to where.

I drive past an eagle sitting on top of a carcass by the side of the road. It seems to make eye contact with me as I drive past. It is glaring at me. For once I get the meaning. Instead of continuing, I stop by the side of the road and phone Victor. He lives in the place I am about to visit. He suggests I stop by and we have a bite to eat.

We do lunch, but I am unable to focus on what he is saying. In his not-much-caring way, he asks how I am. I begin to explain it is as if I have a presence travelling with me. He goes quiet. Most of the time he doesn't listen to anything I say, but this time he does. He leans closer and takes my hand.

He asks me when and where this started. I don't understand what he is asking but when pressed I remember the woman with the necklace I had met in the mall out west.

"This needs to be dealt with," he says. "What else do you have to do today?"

I don't hear the end of his question. My head has hit the table. I can no longer sit up. She is standing very close next to me. It is almost as though she were me. Her yellow dress is damp and grubby. The red kerchief is down around her neck. Her black hair is flung all over the place. She swings the empty flagon at Victor. Instinctively, he blocks it. He slaps both hands flat on the table, scrapes his chair back and rises.

"This had better stop and soon. We don't have much time." He says as he turns to leave and go back to work.

"Come back tonight!" he commands.

I meet up with Victor again in the evening. We drive urgently to a remote location.

"Here!" he says, indicating a dirt track. I screech to a halt and turn off the main road onto the dirt track. We travel on for about half a kilometer down this track until he again points and says, "Here!"

I stop the car. He jumps out in a manner I find uncharacteristic; it makes me think how little I actually know him.

"Wait here!" he says and dashes off into the trees.

He returns minutes later dragging behind him a large branch and some twigs.

"Lucky," he says, "I was concerned there would be none of this tree left here."

He heaps them all up and lights them. A smoky fire puffs into existence. He begins to talk to me fervently. I can't understand much of what he is saying but nod when it seems I am meant to.

He makes me take off my clothes—am I making this up now? I can't remember if I take off my clothes because he asks me to or because that's what I feel I need to do. He shoves my head down into the smoke. He keeps up his talking, telling me what he is doing, talking to the Country round about, to the ghosts who are watching what we are doing, pacifying them and the drunk woman who stands as if part of me yet, beside me.

My eyes start smarting. I begin to cough. I struggle, trying to get back up, but he holds me there, my head in the smoke, until I fall over.

At this point, all else fades. I am part of the landscape surrounded by smoke, sticks and grasses. There is no distinction between the earth and me. I am a stick fallen from a tree. I am a clump of dirt. A stone. Someone wanders over and picks me up, turns me over and over in the palm of their hand. I feel the fingers around me as I am turned. I shudder as I am struck by another stone. I am being sharpened, my edges honed. I am tossed aside. I lie there and feel how I am a stone. I feel the rain run off my surface.

I feel the sun, the moon—time.

I feel silence.

Numbness. Tiny puffs of breeze. Heat. Cold. Black.

Time.

Stillness. Crackling. Rustling. Movement. Time.
Foetal. Standing. Falling. Time.

And then we are back at Victor's home. I am tucked into bed, a cup of peppermint-smelling tea in my hand, the thick smell of smoke all around me. My hands feel dry and cracked. They are streaked with dirt. But they are warm around the cup of tea.

I can tell immediately that the drunken woman has gone. I am alone. The first time in a while. It feels strange to be on my own again.

I fall asleep and I begin to dream. I can remember who I am again. I feel meek and mild—my usual "me."

In the morning, I sit up and ask Victor what happened. He says it must have been the beads the woman had given me at the mall.

"It was a ghost," Victor explains. "You brought it back with you and it was slowly moving in on you. We seem to have got to it in time. She won't bother you anymore."

CROSSING BOUNDARIES

THERE ARE BOUNDARIES and Countries here my immigrant relatives were ignorant of.

My German great great great grandfather was constantly crossing boundaries he was unaware of— between Aranda Country, where he established the Hermannsburg mission, and Bethany, where he settled his wife and family when they arrived from Germany.

In Theodore Strehlow's book, *Journey to Horseshoe Bend*, I read and re-read the sections mentioning my great great great grandfather, hoping for a sign that he recognized and worked with the local Aboriginal peoples, that he learned from the Arranda people, that he began to take notice of the knowledge Aboriginal peoples had, that he eventually found out when he was crossing into another's territory and knew the relevant protocols. I never found any signs that this was the case. I feel ashamed that I am tied to his blindness.

I do feel compassion for my great great great grandmother, about whom I know very little. She must have felt small and frightened in this immense, unknown place. She stayed in Bethany to keep house while my great great great grandfather walked off into the blue of sky and red of earth with his sheep and his religious principles.

She would have been surrounded by women in a similar position. She would have been homesick. When she sent letters home to Germany, how could she have explained the place where she was or what her life was like? Did she have the words to describe it? Would those back home in Germany have had any idea of what she was talking about? What questions would they have asked?

Being the first time you sit to stitch:
    You settle down to remember home.
    You know this feeling of sitting in front of a fire, but in the past it was always with others.
    Still, your body relaxes into the warmth.
    The thread catches in the fabric for a moment, then pulls evenly through.

Being the second time:
    You are stitching the mountain you see when you open the front door.
    You are thinking of the mountain at home, the one everyone at home will be looking at.
    The mountain you see through the front door is not the mountain you stitch.
    The threads tangle at the back of the fabric, tracking where you would prefer to be.

Being the third time:
    You notice that your work is tighter than usual, tiny stitches puckering the fabric.
    As you see this, the stitches get tighter still, the needle squeaks through the fabric.

Your hand is clammy: your eyes tear.

The tears falls onto the fabric: the colors run into each other.

You set aside your work. Everything is quiet. The fire barely flickers.

Being the fourth time:

You take up your work.

You take a deep slow breath to make a sound in the silence.

The days stretch longer than the thread, longer than the journey here.

The fabric you are working on is overly matted. The thread is frayed.

You prick your finger one too many times.

There are blood droplets on the piece.

You hate this work.

You hate this place.

Being the fifth time, being nothing else to be remembered by, you take another breath.

You take up your work. You look at it carefully.

You are rational and calm.

It is awful. You hate it.

You undo the stitches, slowly, measuredly.

Things change soon and you are ripping at the fabric.

Anger welling. Tears welling.

Being the sixth time, you start again.

You take a breath.

You remember home….

The locations most Germans settled in when they arrived in South Australia were almost familiar, almost German-like, or so they seem now, with soft green hills and vines growing over timber and wire trellises. The Germans set about busily making this alien place like home. It must have been hard work and they mostly failed to notice there were other people, the original inhabitants, watching them with curiosity and at times horror. For the Germans undid what the original inhabitants had achieved over a vast length of time, failing to appreciate or understand what was needed to live here in accord with the land.

I so wish that after he had been into the interior of the land, my great great great grandfather found, like me, that he loved the red dirt country which surrounds the Hermannsburg Mission. I wish that he too felt more himself there, as I do. I wish that somehow he intuitively knew and respected Aboriginal peoples, that he saw that they understood more than he ever would or could about the place, the Country they love.

But I know none of this is true.

If I ever watch Aboriginal women painting, I marvel at how long it must have taken them to have learnt so much about their Country; how it is only now when some of them are in wheelchairs and can no longer get around easily that they are able to do what they are doing. They know Country from stories about her, of seeing her in all seasons, in drought, in flood, seeing her with others, being alone with her, through time spent walking on her in bare feet, letting the goodness of the earth get into them, by lying on her, by knowing their body in space, as an extension of that space into the earth, into Country. And it is only after all of this time and experience of being at home there, in place, in body, in spirit, that they begin to know her so they can paint her thus.

Hearing but Not Listening to Country

THE FIRST TIME I VISITED Adnyamantha Country, the Country started to sing. I was in a minibus with my own bunch of strangers I had met only a few hours earlier. We were heading into the Flinders Ranges to a shearing shed on a property to look at "place," specifically to look at "creating in place." We were a mixed bunch of writers, visual artists and a musician.

I mentioned a few times to the others around me that I could hear the Country singing.

"Can you hear it?" I asked. But I did so quietly. I wanted to keep hearing the song and I felt self-conscious. How can you make up such a thing? Everyone continued to look straight ahead as though in fear of me.

I said it again a little louder this time. I needed some confirmation of this wildly exciting experience of the Country singing! Still no one seems to hear me, or no one says anything.

How does Country sing? I will explain what I heard.

Country hums. It is very clear. It hums long, low and tunefully. "Welcome", it says. "Welcome, we see you!"

We continued driving in the minibus and the humming/singing was no longer there—or at least I could no longer hear it.

Everyone continued talking and laughing and having a good time.

I was again amidst their chatter in a bus with a driver who was someone I had admired for some time. The driver had written one of my favorite books.

I so wanted to impress him.

I felt foolish.

But I did hear it.

The story as it is told, the story most white people in Australia understand as "the truth," is that Australia was "discovered" in 1770 and used for prisoners from England. Other peoples from other European lands later began to arrive in this new country. Having taken over the country, the strangers set out in groups to explore the extents of their new territory. Most of these strangers expected to find great riches and to make their fortune so they could go back to their families in their home countries—which were to them, the real countries.

A smaller group of these strangers expected to meet people who already lived in the new land and to change them. To make them realize that there was only one way to be and believe, and it was the strangers' way: the one way, the only way, the way the strangers said things ought to be.

None of the strangers knew or cared about who they might meet here, or what these people might be able to teach them. The strangers knew everything already so there was not much anyone else could teach them.

The strangers lumped all the people in their new territories into one group and called them "Aborigines" although there were over three hundred separate Nations and each of these Nations had their own ways of being and knowing—their own languages, their own customs, their own lives.

The strangers saw the Aborigines in the area where they were and presented this specific, local information as general truth, as in "All Aborigines do this," when it was in fact a local custom, specific only to that one Nation. No distinction was made among Nations or groups. Torres Strait Islanders were unknown.

If you look at a map of Australia showing the different languages spoken (and these are distinctly different languages) you can see how inaccurate and misleading this is. The people who spoke each language had their own customs and ways of being, of knowing and doing; they were in fact distinct Nations. This is only one result of colonization and European imperialism that Aboriginal peoples have been trying to explain to non-Aboriginal people ever since invasion.

One stranger who did this generalized picturing of Aborigines was Carl Strehlow (1871–1922). Carl Strehlow set out to explain the word of God to people in Australia. He replaced my great great great grandfather in 1892 as the head of the Hermannsburg Mission.

Strehlow spent his early time in Australia first at Killalpaninna Mission and then at Hermannsburg, translating Christian texts into local languages. He recorded the local languages and ways of living. Strehlow realized the people he was meeting had a rich knowledge of place very different to his own and he took to translation and ethnographic work, recording what he saw with enthusiasm. Many of his notes are now being used to recover lost, or more accurately, suppressed ways of life of the Arrenda people as they begin to recover their original way of life.

Carl's son, Theodore, later became a figure of controversy. He claimed that he held substantial local

Arrenda knowledge because he had grown up in a remote part of Australia with Arrenda people. He generalized this to all Aboriginal peoples.

He was trusted enough to be given many sacred objects to protect. These objects he claimed were given to him personally and they were therefore—in the European's way of doing things—his to keep. It was only after extensive court cases and expenditures that these objects were returned to their real owners, the Arrenda people.

My great great great grandfather left Bethany which was Peramangk land in January 1876 to establish a mission in Arrenda country. He met up with two other men named Kempe and Schwartz. Disheartened by heat and exhaustion, they struggled on to Dalhousie Springs, then to Adnyamantha Country. They stopped for six months at Witjira so the sheep and horses and cattle they had brought with them could graze and drink water. They were still 300 miles from their destination. After their rest, they moved through:

Dhirari Country
Arabana Country
Antakarinja Country
Arrenda
and Luritja.

It was in Arrenda country that they established Hermannsburg Mission.

Reading about their journey, there is constant talk of their struggle and distress. There is never mention of any assistance they received, but surely there must have been assistance. Did a local guide take them to the best places for water and grazing, show them how to behave? Did they know whose Country they were in at any point?

Did they ever feel an essence of place, a singing under their feet?

Because it is true that other people besides me have felt the singing.

Each of the Countries the strangers walked through has its own language, its own protocols, its own culture, its own Dreamings. At the borders between these Countries, there are official protocols. People are welcomed. Everyone knows how to respond at these crossovers. But these invaders didn't even notice they had crossed a boundary. They failed to wait to be welcomed. They blundered through, oblivious.

Each Country's people watched these pale idiots with their strange beasts. At times, they stepped out of the shadows of their Country to help. The strangers seemed grateful when this happened. They were unable to read any of the signs. They didn't seem to have any idea of where to look for water—maybe they didn't need water? Nor did they know where there might be different plants to eat or where to dig for food. Yet the strangers had taken over their Country.

They had belonged to their Country for—the number of years is contested, but for tens and tens of thousands of years. They had tenderly cared for it, sung to it, painted it, danced for it, loved it, and now they stood powerless and watched as strangers who knew nothing moved in.

I have been to some of the Countries my great great great grandfather crossed. Too often I forget, or fail to recognize, or have some other excuse as to why I didn't acknowledge Country as I crossed into another place. The Elders shake their heads.

EDGES

IT IS AT THE EDGES that so many things occur. The world is a different place through half closed eyes. You block out just enough. You see the feathering of your eyelashes. You see a thin intense strip of life.

On the edges it takes effort not to fall. You step forward, eyes half shut, arms feeling out before you, not knowing exactly where your feet will land. Maybe the ground will remain there, solid under your feet. Or you may fall into an abyss.

The world is filled with edge places if you know where to look. They include motels, caravan parks, verandas, edges of towns, edges of coasts, the edge of the world. These are places where people have landed temporarily: the in-betweeners, people who are restless, who are not clear if they want to stay or move on. They are exploring and are not clear if they will settle down or not. They are in between a proper life, one with a family in a nice house they are paying off from salaried employment, and a life not yet imagined. They are heading nowhere and staying here only for this moment. Because they are in between, a definition is difficult.

They include the Google maps man driving relentlessly across the outback of Australia making maps of the country so that someone in their BMW or Mercedes venturing out this way will have a map to follow. They are the contractors roaming from job to job, location to location, with skills the locals may not possess, working on large infrastructure projects—perhaps installing a pipeline crossing the Country so the Internet can get to the other side.

They are people like myself looking for something about which I am not clear.

The weather can seem as though it is different on the edges—cooler or hotter. Without many structures around, the air moves more freely. There is a chance to make larger motions, fling oneself around to see what happens next.

On the edges, you are out of sight. The people driving don't notice you as they look forward to their destination. They slowed through town, now they see the speed unlimit sign and can take off fast again. They are focused elsewhere and the fact there are people living on the edge of the town fails to register. Everyone in town knows there are people out there but it slips to the edge of their attention.

In Australia, everyone wants a veranda around their house—an edge between the house and the outside world. On the veranda, you can sit and watch others without being seen.

Once, an in-betweener between houses, between jobs, I slept in an old timber house amidst rolling green hills. I was staying with a friend. The room she let me have had no windows, only glazed doors, which opened directly onto a verandah. The bed was positioned so it looked out through the doors and across the width of the veranda to the fields beyond.

I felt as though I were an invalid. In the mornings I would lie in bed with the thick hand-knitted blankets weighing me down and watch my hostess training her horses. After she returned from her chores and I had risen, we would sit together on the veranda to drink coffee. Her clothes were already sweaty. My nightie was still warm from the bed.

Her chores were never done. Mine never started. All I did was read slowly through the huge of piles of books I had brought with me until I reached the book at the bottom. I sat then for some time longer in the cool of the veranda. My vision was stopped above by its decorative frieze, blocked below by the dense balusters of the handrail. When I felt I could no longer justify my sitting there in silence and shade, I took to the fields with her, always making sure I could place the dark line of the veranda—a line describing its coolness and repose—at the edge of my vision.

All about the house, it was lush and cool. Things grew everywhere. The house moved outwards from its heart-thick-walled internal dark rooms, lighter timber rooms edging this, a delicate line of the veranda edging this, the garden edging the veranda, the fields edging the garden, the hills edging the fields, the sea edging the hills, the rest of the world edging the sea.

I finally had to leave.

THREADS

A Map for Country

Sitting in a gallery, I am watching a screen upon which women assemble at the edges of a large canvas. They are at ease with each other. They have an aura of quiet excitement. They are going to paint a map of their Country. Each woman will paint the part she knows physically, emotionally and spiritually. Together they will fill a painting so large that once it is finished and ready for transporting to the exhibition space, it will take several men to haul the three meters high by five meters long canvas onto the back of a truck.

I wonder what it might be like to belong so strongly to a place. To know a place so well that you can paint it from memory. To know a place so well that you feel it in your body. When there is drought, you too are parched; when it is mined, you too feel dug out, disfigured. The women belong to the Country they are painting. I watch them in the video as they approach the canvas and prepare to paint. They are chatting. I don't understand what it is they are saying, but it is clear they are discussing what they are about to paint—where they will start, how they will place Country on the canvas. They speak as though they are discussing a dear friend. And they are, of course. They are there to paint her portrait.

They continue talking as they take their places, sit down and begin. They are scattered around the edges of the canvas as though randomly but each has knowing intent. Each woman paints her portion of the Country, her story. Together they compose a symphony, knowing as they paint that what each is painting will combine to produce something greater than herself. Each woman is painting a phrase, a melody extending across the continent of Australia, end to end, west to east, together becoming something extraordinary.

Over the time the painting takes for them to complete, they drift to and from the canvas; sometimes losing interest; sometimes needing a smoke; or maybe they need to go and attend to a funeral or there is a relative who needs assistance; they return when they are ready to continue.

Traveling to the Exhibition

I have come to this exhibition with my friend, Katerina. Katerina is from Europe and while knowledgeable about many things she doesn't have the background I have of growing up in Australia. She doesn't know the things I do about the country—things you don't even think to list since you fail to appreciate that others do not know them. Things such as Christmas time will be bloody hot, no need to wonder about that. You can rely on going for a swim after eating a huge Christmas meal: a mix of roast turkey, roasted vegetables, fresh rock oysters and local prawns: followed by plum pudding, a strawberry pavlova and ice cream, having along the way the obligatory argument on whether a pav is an Australian or a New Zealand invention. Or knowing you don't swim in the evenings since that is shark feeding time. Or to check before you put your hand into the shed to switch on the light to make sure there are no redback spiders lurking there.

The exhibition is being held in a place I once called home. I attended high school here, but I left to go to university in the city—then a five-hour drive, but now, after mammoth road improvements, an easier but more boring drive of three and a half hours to the northeast. I have lived in the city ever since. The city is now my "home." These two places are kilometers apart both in distance and mindset—one is a place where my mother would wonder on our return from holidays if someone had dropped an atomic bomb while we were away, decimating everyone, since there was never a soul about; the other a place of constant activity and street life, including the millions of cockroaches scuttling around.

Katerina and I catch the coach to the exhibition at the crack of dawn. The coach drops us at a bus station on the main street in the center of town. From there we walk to the museum, which is located on the edge of a lake comparatively close by.

After fording expressways and roads, I notice a dirt track cutting closer to the lake's shores which will make the route slightly shorter. I take off across the grass, anxious to be at the exhibition. Katerina hesitates on the path before reminding me of the possibility of snakes, something that has not crossed my mind. I never do think of snakes, except perhaps when bushwalking with a group of others. I know it is best to walk heavily, to be as noisy as possible and to jump on top of a log rather than over it, to give the snakes a chance to feel your vibration and get away.

It is the sort of day snakes like, hot and dry, and I should have thought about the possibility of snakes being out and about. Katerina, like most travelers to Australia, is very aware of them and has been told not only about the numerous and extremely dangerous snakes and spiders but also about the sharks, crocodiles, and drop bears. These creatures are constantly on the alert for opportunities to savage you.

Australians delight in telling stories which start with, "Did you hear about the time when…?" The pregnant woman bitten as she leaves her car. The man, who without hesitation, chops off his finger with a machete so that the venom can't travel to the rest of his body. The female funnel-web spider a friend's father discovers under his pillow which he remembers vaguely brushing off in the middle of the night. The night I myself wake to something heavy walking across the bed to find a palm-sized mouse-eating spider. Huntsmen spiders. Huntsmen jumping. Huntsmen playing dead so the cat loses interest and leaves it alone and then suddenly springing back to life again. Huntsmen on the left-hand side of the bed as you close your eyes and then on the right-hand side of the bed when you open them a few minutes later. A million huntsmen spider stories.

Millions more snake stories. Someone said no one in Australia is ever more than ten meters away from a snake, even in the major cities. Despite knowing all this, I say to Katerina, "No, no snakes. Besides," I add, "the grass has just been cut and we will see them before they see us and if we walk noisily, they will be scared off."

Katerina had been to Canberra earlier in the year to see an exhibition of paintings curated from work produced along the length of the Canning Stock Route, a route through the desert connecting water places so non-Indigenous people could move cattle from one place to another. The Canning Stock Route is claimed to be the longest stock route in the world. Indigenous and non-Indigenous lives have not always intersected easily along its length. It is a route about which stories by non-Indigenous people have become legendary. It is a route about which Indigenous stories have rarely been heard. The Canning Stock Route was made by a non-Indigenous person who failed to recognize its 1,850 kilometers disrupted many cultural boundaries. The Canning Stock Route (Yiwarra Kuju) exhibition set out to change this and to give an Indigenous voice to the stock route's history.

Katerina had been overwhelmed by what she saw at the Yiwarra Kuju exhibition. It was she who convinced me to come along to the Songlines: Tracking the Seven Sisters exhibition.

We are each on a mission even though we each have a slightly different one. I want to explore this place, this country, my home, and my relationship to it. Katerina wants to explore ways of being in a place which is not her home, but is a place she wants to make her home. Both of us want to explore ways of knowing about place, other than through European sensibilities. In Australia we are taught to see and hear things the ways Europeans do. We assume these ways of seeing and being are "normal"— even the only and best way.

European descriptions of public or shared space are often external and structured. The plaza and piazza are distinctly defined by buildings of a certain scale and form. The private ways of knowing place, through smells, tastes, sounds, association, or the intuitive connection with place, may be less often shared, more a matter for poetry, song, private memory.

When the English arrived in Australia, they failed to notice the destruction they were causing, despite being told repeatedly by those already here, because they were looking for things, places, buildings, environments to be the same as what they had "at home" in England. The English made the place into a replica of all things English, perhaps because of their nostalgia, but at any rate, ignoring the idea that there might be a different way and that this different way might be appropriate here.

We hoped the Songlines exhibition would give us a chance to see differently, outside of our usual ways of seeing things and that as a consequence, our understandings of "place" would deepen.

SONGLINES: TRACKING THE SISTERS

When we finally arrived at the exhibition space, we stepped into a darkened lobby. We were met by the sound of raindrops falling.

The sound of rain has taken on a significance it might not have had in previous decades. Rain means lushness and coolness—a release after a long spell of drought. When rain starts after a long time without it, it is as though everything—people, flora, fauna, Country—stops to listen and breathes a sigh of contentment.

Light puddled in concentric circles on the carpet in front of us. These concentric circles began to morph into abstract shapes at the same time as the rain gradually morphed into the sound of Aboriginal women singing. Cleansed, we stepped through an open glass sliding door into the exhibition space and walked past abandoned wheelchairs to the first of the paintings.

Amazing paintings…and more amazing paintings… more and more amazing paintings.

Life size people on banners saying "Welcome" in each of their different languages.

Pieces of pottery to explain the stories to children.

A canvas made with felt pieces cut out and stuck to produce a "dot" painting, subverting the more usual way people imagine Aboriginal paintings.

Flying sculptures of seven mermaids, their feet tied together at the ends, their arms in loops over their head as though pirouetting.

A photograph of a cave with the eyes of a god, watching as you walk past.

Videos of women singing and telling stories.

A room with a huge painting, "Yarrkalpa," on one wall. On the opposite wall, a video of the eight women painting it. On the third wall, a video with alternating clips of the surrounding landscape and close up shots of the dresses of the women painting. On the last wall, a video of over-sized dingoes panting in the heat.

The Songlines: Tracing the Seven Sisters exhibition is a collection of paintings, stories, sculptures, pottery and made objects, a journey across three Australian deserts through the country of the Martu, the Anangu, Ptjantjarara, Yankunytjatjara (APY lands) and the Ngaanyatjarra peoples. The Seven Sisters story is a Songline. It is a part of the Dreaming.

The terms Songline and Dreaming remain contested. Professor Larissa Behrendt, an Eualeyai/Kamillaroi woman, a legal academic and writer, defines Songlines as routes taken for cultural exchange of ideas, songs, and ceremonies between nations, often following Dreaming tracks. She goes on to explain that the Dreaming "is the name given to the period when the world was created, with spiritual ancestors journeying across the landscape along dreaming tracks, creating its features, central to Aboriginal worldviews and spirituality." The two concepts, Songlines and the Dreaming, are ones non-Indigenous people have grappled with, trying to understand them but never fully getting there.

It is only two hundred and thirty years since Australia was colonized, taken as a *terra nullius*, and these concepts of songlines and the Dreaming had been forming for many thousands of years. They are essential to the Aboriginal and Torres Strait Islander peoples' world views. It does not matter what non-Indigenous people make of them.

The Seven Sisters—as people, as landforms, as stars— are pursued endlessly by a sorcerer, and in the course of this pursuit, stories are told; landscape is formed; earth is made into Country. Each group of people has their own stories and Country. They hand the line from one group to the next group over the boundary of their Country, working in collaboration with each other.

One function of the Songlines in some places at some times is as a mnemonic—a way to remember landscape features and to locate oneself in those features; to make the place, to sing Country to oneself. The Seven Sisters are of course also stories, as all people have told stories forever. If necessary, they can provide a deeper explanation of subjects that cannot always be told directly. The songlines as revealed in the exhibition are subtle and beautiful.

The Seven Sisters' Songline rises on the west coast and continues to the east coast, the expanse of Australia. In this exhibition, parts of the songlines, Dreamtime and stories of the three nations of people that they are able to reveal are told. Some of the paintings continue off the canvas to lead those who know and understand to unseen things. These unseen things are things that cannot be said or shown to those who cannot be told the full story. The sisters, therefore, disappear into waterholes, move off the canvas to do things off stage and then re-appear elsewhere on the canvas. Or maybe in a cave. Perhaps inside Walinynga Cave or Cave Hill on the APY lands. Who knows.

Walinynga Cave is one of the most significant rock art sites in Australia. Here there are layers upon layers of paintings done over thousands of years. When Walinynga Cave was opened it up to the public, the custodians painted yellow concentric circles over the parts not to be viewed by outsiders. "Look, here, at the bits we can't show you!"

The Seven Sisters appear in the landscape as rocks or as trees and then spring to the sky to disappear from winter to summer. They dive into the ground to hide from the sorcerer who has been following them.

Exhausted, Katerina and I both fell immediately asleep on the coach trip home.

When we met up a week later, we decided to pursue placemaking in more detail. Did the exhibition change at all how we had thought about place and our place in that place? Did it change at all our way of being in a place? What about our sense of how those places might be bounded? How might we map this place where we are right now and how we arrived here?

We decided to start by exploring a single painting from the exhibition. We would try to understand the place it maps and how it was made. We would attempt to know its boundaries through our boundaries, through

Country's boundaries, through space, time and place, through architecture, through the Japanese concept of *ma* space and time, a sense of place, through writing's boundaries.

YARRKALPA

We decided to work on one painting, Yarrkalpa (Hunting Ground), by a collective of Martumili women artists— the painting we had watched a video of as the women painted country.

In the catalogue of the exhibition, Yarrkalpa (Hunting Ground) takes up two full pages. Stills from a video show the eight Martumili women and their process of painting Yarrkalpa. To determine the limits and layout of the painting, the women discuss where the "creek beds" (white lines in the painting) should be placed and where the limits of the painting should be.

They decided to start with water, their Country's blood and lifeline. And of course it is for us all. The rest of the painting flows once the water lines are in place.

Each part of the painting shows an intense and intimate knowledge of Country as well as many of the local traditional practices such as burning, tracking and gathering. These practices are explained in a commentary handwritten on a tracing paper overlay. This overlay also locates sand hills, places where wattles grow, where native food plants grow, where there is black ash that is good for tracking goannas, clay pans, where the wind has blown so hard there is no growth, grevilleas, bush plums, white coolibah, the community oval, grasslands, gullies, where the Seven Sisters sat and from where they were watched, the place to find green parrot flower bark to make bush sandals, the Parngurr community location.

The painting women are grounded and earthy, focused; absorbed. This is what they know. There are no hesitations. They seem clear on the boundaries between each other, between their Country and the Country of the woman sitting adjacent to them. The painting shows these boundaries. There is no blurring between them—I know here: you know there.

These boundaries, these breaks between here and there, represent edges not obvious to anyone else from outside this Aboriginal nation. Most of us might look for a riverbank or cliff edge, a distinct change of material or an obvious gap. Mostly we remain oblivious to the boundaries shown in Yarrkalpa. Here there are ghosts of rivers or creek beds. Slight inclines which may have been former hills. Places where white coolibah grows on what was once a river flat. Here the honey grevillea. There, a clay pan. Each woman has a knowledge of a subtle land where much more can be seen if you know the place intimately enough and can "read" it. Only when you "know" Country like this can you paint it in this way.

The colors and patterns, names and plants and landscape features are overwhelming and I want to understand it, to colonize it, to make it a place I know too. At the same time, I try not to do this. I try to let them *be*—as I might in meditation or aikido, labelling my attempts at understanding simply *thoughts*.

I try to let the painting's warp and weft pass through me.

The painting has no linear narrative or at least none I can see. To seek a narrative seems to miss the point.

Instead, there is a half Easter egg with rick-racked patterns across its middle.

There are sections of stripes, crooked stripes, like the raked areas of pebbles in Zen gardens—order in disorder, careful placement, carefulness in the disrupted earth.

Maybe the painting is a Moroccan bazaar. The stall owners lay out their wares for you to browse through. You can walk for miles among these wares—each one more intense and richer than its neighbor, tantalizing you, ensuring you move further and further amongst unknown things until you are lost.

A radiance of color, texture and shapes. There are patterns and tiny thin orderly strokes as well as bold thick ones. Dots. Stripes. Zig-zags. Concentric shapes. You keep walking on, out, through, over, up, as a cacophony of things pulls you on. On and on your eyes move until they reach the perimeter where you shift from one leg to the other and your vision takes off again to roam the painting back to the other edge.

A lot of the painting has been covered over by tiny white dots, giving these sections a delicacy and lightness—a feathery-ness, a shimmering.

At the top left of the painting are seven circles. These represent the seven sisters sitting in a row commanding the entire painting. Just below waits Yurlu, the stalker in this Country, watching them. There is a water hole close by to drink from, to disappear into if need be.

Moving further away from the Seven Sisters, down and across the painting, there are trees laid out as you might expect in an Egyptian painting with their limbs and branches laid down in elevation on either side of a pathway between them.

The eye travels ceaselessly over the painting, stopping here at the red and pink and orange before being pulled over there to the green, more green and yellow. The boundaries between each part are distinct. Each delineated clearly. Each representing very different things. I wonder whether I would recognize the place if I were to drive there or fly over it. I look at the aerial photos of this land when I Google it and I cannot see the features so clearly mapped in the painting. It is my inability to comprehend the Country's subtlety, my inability to "see" Country at all.

I try to relate this painting to things I am familiar with.

Suddenly I see, or imagine I see, a space man stamped onto the landscape.

Over there is a plant in its tightening pot.

It is like looking at the stars with its clusters, smears of light and space: like looking at silence, the space like rests in music, as important to the music as notes of sound.

While I was in architecture school, one of my lecturers explained you can only see to the extent of the spread of your two hands placed together, fingers splayed, all ten outstretched. When I say this to others, they seem uninterested, but I often check diagrams and plans this way—what can I read as a whole, what can I comprehend with a single gaze without moving my head.

When I look at the painting, I wonder how these seated women have painted together something as large as this. They sat on top of the canvas and painted all around themselves. Did they need to hold the whole painting, the whole country in their minds as they painted? Perhaps they had no need to. Perhaps they know each other to trust they will each paint as true a representation of the Country as possible.

I spread my hands out, palms down, fingers widespread. The space is wider than my laptop's keyboard, wider than an open paperback, almost exactly as wide as the Songlines: Tracking the seven sisters catalogue. Could I ever know a place well enough that I could paint it into a space condensed into my two outstretched hands?

RECOGNITION

THE THREE OF US have been driving for over a day. This is the furthest away from our office we have ever ventured together. We are off to attend a Community Meeting and will afterwards speak with the people present to find out not only how things are going generally in town but also to get an understanding of how the funding allocated to the town might best be spent. A major part of our work is to inspect the community's existing houses, audit what needs to be done on each to improve the living conditions, and develop a program of works.

This last task has been done by many other groups of mixed-skill public servants over the years. Each group heads off enthusiastically and returns with their ideas pretty much formed on the drive back home. Few listen to what the people within the town have to say.

We have been told that above all we should listen to what people have to say. When we are told this, as one we nod our heads. It sounds easy, but listening and being directed by others isn't always easy. We nod our heads and intend to listen, but do we really? What if what they have to say is not what we want to hear? What if it challenges everything we think we know? Still, we nod our heads and think *Yep, we will definitely be different from all the others.*

People in the office warn us that nothing will prepare us for what this particular town is like. Katy and I joke about this in the car as we get closer and closer: Enjoy that hamburger, that drink, those chips, that cheerful feeling—it could be your last for some time. I am leaning towards the front seat where Katy sits and Keith is driving. There are various chip and other empty packages strewn around my feet. It is stuffy in the car. Although the air conditioning is turned up high, it is hot in here, particularly in the back where the cooler air barely reaches.

As we approach our destination, I am wondering why this town is located where it is. Reading its history doesn't help. Mostly these histories refuse to recognize anything except colonizing history and overlook the longer history, the local Aboriginal peoples' history, a more physical, bodily history, which has located the town with notions of the aliveness of the surrounding country and its importance in relationship to the Dreaming and other essential ideas.

This town is almost equidistant between two larger towns but it is close to none. There are no doubt complex reasons for its location here, reasons other than the obvious ones of access to water and services. The town's recent past has been brutal and tragic, so perhaps it is not really meant to be here at this location on the river at all. People say strange things happen here—the inhabitants see into you, stare at you at length until they can see who you are, your weaknesses, your strengths, your identity, where you belong.

With my mind drifting I wonder what border is crossed to delineate between "in town" and "not in town." Is it as obvious as the speed limit sign making a threshold without which we would never know we were "there?"

At the moment we arrive, I am looking at the horizon and how the colors of earth and sky mix and I am planning the cloak I will make from it.

From here on the edge of town, everything appears to be floating. It is a shimmering mirage with no ropes tying it to the earth. There are colonial buildings. Many are made from local stone and clay. They snake along the river. The place once boasted it was the largest inland port in Australia; it had paddle steamers carrying passengers and materials up and down the river, or so I have heard. Now most people speed through the place in their air-conditioned cars, with a few pausing for any length of time or glancing left or right, afraid of what they might see there.

The landscape's immensity is echoed by its silence, which roars unendingly. There is the pounding of the earth below, the huge sky booming above. Here, you are always aware of your insignificance as you stand like a thin watercolor dribble between earth and sky.

The horizon is dead straight. Red below. Blue above. Hawks and eagles circle between sky and earth. Roos and emus wander about. What's left of the river is slow and sullen and twists through the land, writhing to a slow painful death. There are enormous trees on the river's edge—at least three people would have to hold each others' hands to wrap their arms around them. The trees have gnarled branches and deeply grooved bark. They are weighed down with heavy hearts, these trees, and bend low to feel the last dribs of the river's water on their leaves. When the river is running fast and smoothly so does the town, but when the river begins to fail, as it does now, so does the town.

Perhaps the town is failing because its settlement history condemns it to fail.

It is not just a place where alcohol, unemployment and destitution triumph—nor is it simply a place where the remains of a sandstone town has been stopped dead in its tracks—although these are certainly essential parts of it. It is not just that, as in many outback country towns, people have left it and moved off the land to be somewhere else, hoping things might miraculously change for them. Because, as in so many other outback towns, there appears nothing much to do here.

The shopkeeper here is also the publican. Agency people drive into town for a day and then drive back home again, and it is easy to find an excuse to skip a day. The larger stakeholders have bought up all the water rights. During droughts, even though massive amounts of water are released down the river from a short distance upstream, the water no longer reaches this place. People claim that on the day the water is released, they can see the river flowing backwards as cotton farmers—the big land holders who own all the water rights up and down the river's edges rush and begin to pump the water to store it in their own storage tanks for their own private usage later.

All these things are true, but they do not distinguish this place from many other towns round about.

This town is almost exclusively an Aboriginal town. In driving through, particularly for those who have come from the big city, it may be the first time they have seen any "real" Aboriginal people, particularly so many Aboriginal people in the one place at the one time. It is unmistakably populated with Aboriginal people where most other towns on the way have managed to hide their original inhabitants.

We have planned our arrival time to be not too early or there will be nothing to do, nor too late for there mightn't be any rooms left in the "good" motel and we will have to stay at the "crazy" one instead. It has to be timed just right.

As we drive into town, everything is quiet. The low-slung verandas and blue stone buildings remind me of my childhood visiting small Barossa Valley towns in South Australia. Towns like Tanunda, Clare, Nurioopta and Bethany are now popular tourist destinations as tourists roam the valley hunting for wine and good food. Those towns are filled with the childhood stories of my mother and her family. Our visits there were scented by the soft peppery smell of feathery leaved trees with pink peppercorns drifting in swirls around us as my grandfather drove up and then down each street in his Chevy.

The town we are visiting now has no memories for me. I have never been here before. What I find is a town with six streets, two pubs, a club, a small supermarket, two motels, a small hospital, a swimming pool and a Shell service station. There is a population of less than 1,000 people. Many of these 1,000 people move from house to house depending on the season but rarely will they move to any other location.

But just as in the Barossa Valley, people cling to the shaded walls, lurking at door openings where a cool breeze can be felt. There they can talk, smoke and drink together in the sweltering heat. No one looks up as Katy,

Keith and I cruise by. They can tell who we are from our car's make: we must be Government employees and so we are of no consequence. The Shell servo is the only place where there is any activity—the screen door opening and slapping shut as people come and go, buying junk foods long past their due-by dates, lukewarm from the bain-marie or fridge.

The town was established in the same year my mother's great great grandfather arrived in Australia from Germany.

We are to meet a fellow worker, Victor, who will help with introductions and any negotiations needed. He set up the Community meeting. He knows lots of the people involved or at least they know of his family, which will help with easing our way into the confidence of the Community. Confidence will only really be developed over time. This will be the first of many visits if we are really to be able to do anything of value here.

We hang around expectantly at the designated meeting spot. We wait…and wait…. Eventually Victor arrives at the meeting spot only a couple of hours late. He is neatly dressed and has also driven a hire car, the same brand, color and model as ours. No doubt he picked it up at exactly the same place. It too is parked on the road. He sits uncomfortably on a picnic table trying to look casual and hip at the same time. He jumps up as we drive alongside, recognizing us as everyone else had, by the car: red, large, new. We are all the same, us Government officials.

We think we are being novel when we decide to give a community barbecue. Great idea, we nod to each other, little knowing that community people joke about how sick they are of sausage—how they are only ever offered sausages at these Government barbecues. How they long for something novel—lamb cutlets for example, or something entirely different, maybe not readily available where they live: haloumi, for example or a Lebanese feast!

We wander over to introduce ourselves. Victor is concerned that he won't be much help to us. He explains he doesn't know the place very well. He's only ever driven through, as he heads back home to his own family, kilometers to the southeast—a different mob altogether, but he'll do what he can to help. We know no matter what, he will give us some element of credibility. The people here are extremely cynical about Government people arriving in town, saying they will listen to what the Community has to say, having a barbecue and then driving out again, having not heard a word of what people want to say.

The people here are used to being frustrated. They are used to everything in their life being a failure. They resolved a long time ago to pile the sausages, salad and bread onto a large plate and run with it back home where they can share it comfortably with the rest of the family. They think that at least they have had a feed tonight, at least this is something. It would, however, be better if something else other than sausages was cooked on the barbie every now and then. That would show the Government people had been listening to them!

The night is still young and time yawns like a publican's throat in front of us. We plan to spend ten minutes or so freshening up, go find something to eat and then afterwards maybe we might think about having a drink somewhere if we feel up to it.

Ten minutes later exactly finds the four of us back out the front of the motel ready for dinner. Victor tells us he'd heard meals were pretty good over at the Club. He adds as an afterthought, though, that the cook went AWOL the week before—no one was sure why, so meals were off there. But, he says, we could take our own food over and cook it in the Club's kitchen. This might be the very best meal to be had in town! Unfortunately, he remembers, the supermarket is now shut and with nowhere else in town to get food this option is also now closed to us.

We'll have to eat at the Shell service station.

It's hard not to feel glum as you stand in front of a bain-marie looking at dead food and trying to work out which of the choices might be the least bad for you. Packaged crisps, ice creams and lollies start looking pretty good. At least you know what the ingredients are. Hot dogs, Chico rolls, limp warm chips. Which would it be? I choose a hamburger figuring although the meat will be greasy and it will be surrounded by a huge white sweet bun, it will have vegetables of a sort (limp lettuce, pale greenish tomato, tinned beetroot) even if they are old.

We sit inside the Shell at one of its grubby Laminex-topped tables, each with our selected food on a paper bag in front of us. We chew and swallow down our meals like cows, staring out at the petrol bowsers. Each bowser is locked securely with a padlock and chain and must be unlocked by an attendant whenever someone requires petrol. The reason is obvious: young children can be seen staggering around out on the street with plastic containers hanging around their necks for sniffing gasoline fumes.

Keith slurps down the last of his milkshake and looks around ready for more.

I leave most of my Fanta. It had been silly to think I had changed and would like it.

(Hours left of the evening.)

"So. What now?" Katy looks hopeful but there isn't much hope to be seen amongst the rest of us.

(Still hours left of the evening.)

"Dunno. I'm not from here. Not much choice really." Victor wipes his hands nervously on his jeans.

We finally leave the Shell and go out to stand by the side of the road. There are the four of us, the sky and nothing more. The enormity of the sky makes it difficult to locate yourself. As you lean your head back to find the Southern Cross, everything begins to spin. You find you are facing south when you thought you were facing north, east when west. The silence in the street is broken occasionally when a road-train thunders through barely slowing although the speed limit is way below what they are travelling. These trucks come out of, and return to, nowhere. The world returns to its silence.

Perhaps, we decide after a bit, we will visit the pub. It has to be found first, though, as this is no ordinary pub. Like the rest of the town, it tends to shape-shift and to move from location to location as the need arises. Publicans change; places fall in and out of favor and the pub shifts location to suit. There is no certainty from day to day where it might be found.

At the moment, the pub is in a small squat building perched on the corner diagonally opposite the Shell. All of its windows are boarded up. The door is shut. To enter, you knock and a small bar-covered peep-hole at the door's center opens so the person inside can check to see who is there. If you pass muster, the door is unlocked by the unseen someone and you can enter. The door is then slammed shut again by an ingenious mechanism operating as an automatic door closer: a steel reinforcing rod tied to a rope inside the door.

Any distinguishing features of the building have been erased from its interior. The stone walls are concrete rendered. There is a concrete floor, which can be cleaned easily by a garden hose. There are no moveable fittings left. Everything that can be hurled has been and then it has been removed or fixed permanently to the floor. In the middle of the room, there is an enclosed timber bar with a laminated countertop. The bar base is bolted to the floor. Its laminated top is bolted to its base. Only the taps to the kegs below are visible. Glasses are kept under the counter in locked cupboards. All alcohol, other than beer, is kept in a locked shut refrigerator in another locked room. It is a drinking bastion, secure in time and place from the outside world. Its lack of features focuses the mind. Within the pub, the only thing to do is drink. There can be no dreaming of other worlds here. Drinking reigns supreme.

We knock. The small window in the door opens. An unseen observer gazes at each of us and then, deemed to be of a suitable character, we are given permission to enter. Once inside, the four of us stand awkwardly together, occupied with our own worries. I find myself imagining what the others are thinking.

Victor isn't certain in what makes him *him*. He is standing awkwardly with these Government officials trying to indicate through body language that he is with us but not really. He knows of course that he represents all

Aboriginal people everywhere to his workmates—a kind of Aboriginal everyman or "No-man" as he jokes with his Aboriginal friends. There is no doubt of his Aboriginality. His mother is a well-known activist in his hometown and he struggled at school with racism. That isn't the issue. It is him.

He feels awkward being him. He has always felt awkward in who he is in everything, so being awkward in his Aboriginality is just one more instance. Here in this town, which is not his town, not his Country even, he worries about how he might seem.

He is not dark skinned and while this usually doesn't matter, here it makes him uneasy. He is new to this Government work and this too is a problem. He enjoys the money. He enjoys the entitlements: the flexible work hours, the superannuation, sick leave, the travel allowance. He enjoys driving around in a large red car—new, clean and powerful, but he worries what it might look like to others, especially to the Aboriginal community who are for the main unlikely to ever have any type of car.

He's always been the *scholarship boy*—more, the *Aboriginal scholarship boy*. He had left home early to board at a fancy school at a larger town up the road. The boarding had been hard at first. He'd missed his family, especially his mum.

But as time went on, it got harder and harder to go home during school holidays. He felt awkward with everyone. So much was expected of him. His family, especially his pop, was so proud of him. He was no longer used to their daily routine. At school, he knew exactly what to do and when. At school, there were the other scholarship boys to talk with. At home, there was pretty much no one.

He stands here now worrying about all of this, worrying whether he will be able to prove himself to both lots of people when the time comes—how can he be on both sides when he isn't sure himself which side he wants to be on?

Katy isn't certain her superiority will be noticed. She is of course more competent, more approachable, more successful, more beautiful than her fellow workers.

She hadn't wanted to come here in the first place and particularly not with Keith and the other woman. She is missing out on a cocktail party at home, one she'd been looking forward to for ages. You need more experience, they had said in the office, if you want to go for any promotion. She might be stuck in that office with that bunch of boring morons for the rest of her life unless she can find some way out of there and having more, and different, experiences will help with this. It is nearly killing her now.

She has a personal crusade to share with others the importance of landscape architecture. She knows how to have a good time. She is smart, or so everyone says, but she knows she needs more field experience. All righty then, she will start collecting experiences.

She looks around the pub and zeroes in on a couple of locals. She will go and chat them up: flirt with them if you like. Nah, too far gone, she decides. She certainly isn't going to hang around with the others for any longer tonight though. She has already spent hours and hours driving with them today and that is more than enough for anyone.

With a cold beer in her hand and money sticking out of her wallet, she sidles over to shout some people a drink. She decides on some people clumped around a small shelf attached to the wall. They look okay and might have something interesting to say. She feels if she can play her cards right, drinks enough, and then some, and is just a little out of control, she might be invited back to someone's house.

She'll show them, stuck up pricks, these fellow workers of hers. By the end of the few days here, she intends to be best buddies with a couple of the locals. She figures if she can do this, any negotiations they do at the meeting in the next day or so will be much easier. She has visions of singing around a campfire or watching footy on a furry telly in a backyard somewhere and having a meal of barbecued roo or emu just as she has read about. Doing any of these things are sure to impress the others.

Keith is worried he is going to have to sit on his one drink all night. He was relieved of course they were at least in a pub, a place he is comfortable in. He is already totally over being with this bunch of people. He thought it was going to be kind of fun when he was told they were coming out this way.

He's done trips like this before but always with men. This time he is stuck with a couple of women: Katy who seems kind of okay but whoa, ambitious or what and the other one he isn't quite sure about her, she is...he isn't sure but she seems kind of....

Anyway, it doesn't really matter much. It seems like he is there for doing the driving and he does like driving—no, that isn't the problem. It is being cooped up in a car with two women. He is having to be so careful about what he says, how he says it, what he does, how he does it. Their idea of a good time certainly isn't the same as his and he feels cramped and dissatisfied.

The two girls frowned when he'd had another drink last night with dinner. I mean, honestly, it was only two beers, what were they, wowsers or something. He'd stopped then. He would have been up for a few more, always up for a few more, he is known for being a good drinker and it had been a long day and all and it is the way he relaxes, a few drinks (who doesn't?) but they had turned to each other after a single glass of wine and said, "Ooooh, I feel so drunk, better get to bed, gotta be in good form for the big drive tomorrow", so he felt sort of obliged to go and flop in his motel room alone and watch telly.

There are still three more days of this! Oh god, how is he going to stand it? Katy has already peeled off some of her clothes and is making a beeline for a group near the bar. He is standing here with the bloke, Victor and the other one, he better find someone or something interesting to do pretty quick smart or he'll be left standing having to entertain one or other of them. Oh my god, how boring can a night be!

For me, any occasion is a good one for worrying. I worry that despite the smallness of the town I find it hard to put all its pieces together and each time there is a turn or crossroad, I seem to choose the wrong direction to go. I worry that I won't be my best for the next day's meeting and no one else in the team will turn up and I will be left in my not-the-best-of-states to run the meeting by myself.

Most of all, I worry that I like the place—that I feel at home here, despite having never been here before and knowing little of the people or its expectations. I had been warned repeatedly it is a hard place, a difficult place, but it's true, I like it here.

Why? I worry.

Elsewhere in the pub, more public dramas are occurring.

The publican is striding amongst his patrons proudly showing his bleeding slit neck, the result of earlier interaction during the day between him and some patrons. There had been a kind of flash riot, riot is perhaps too strong a word, more a brawl—a result of too much alcohol and the heat. It hadn't been too serious but it had left the publican holding a huge handkerchief to his throat to stop the blood. People ooh and aah as he walks amongst them.

He feels justified in closing the doors to the pub ceremoniously and only letting in people in dribs and drabs. He feels triumphant in the knowledge that the people he refuses entry to will have nowhere else to go for the evening, failing to recognize that his livelihood depends on there being a continuous flow of alcohol available for everyone. He fails to appreciate he can't be as wealthy as he is without people buying alcohol. It is in his interest to have the whole town in an alcoholic stupor.

After the publican has stood amongst his patrons and they have admired his wound, everyone returns to drinking. Everyone resumes their raving about nothing in particular in voices of increasing volume with less and less likelihood of listening to anything said by anyone else.

I know people see my silence as being defiant and sullen, but it is actually from shyness, uncertainty and lack of confidence. I find crowds of people difficult. I am self-conscious. I find one or two people much easier. In a pub, I can be overwhelmed by so many people—and here I knew none of them.

I should have realized the only resource capable of being shared in a pub, apart from bonhomie, is alcohol. I should have taken part in the drinking in some form or another. In a town of drinkers not drinking is like throwing down a gauntlet. But I failed to recognize this. I refused the offer of a drink—any drink at all—alcoholic or not—not even water would I accept.

The other thing I can be is stubborn.

For whatever reason, on this occasion I decided to be stubborn and continued to refuse any offers of drinks.

This was probably seen as uppity, downright rude. The person who had asked me whether I wanted a drink had maybe never received this type of refusal before. And as a visitor, I was no doubt expected to be good for a couple of shouts and here I was refusing to co-operate. I could easily have asked for a lemonade or a lemon, lime and bitters or water even and joked about being on the wagon and begun yarns of my drinking prowess. Then I would be expected to offer everyone else a drink again and again. This would have satisfied everyone instead I merely kept saying, "No thanks. I'm right—thank you," in my best polite voice and refusing to engage with anyone.

Not a good way to make friends in a Drinking Town.

But the people in this town didn't give up easily. They too were stubborn. I was asked again. And again. And again. Questioned repeatedly given the opportunity to co-operate and act properly. Why wasn't I drinking? Why didn't I want a drink? The answer, "Because I am not really thirsty" seemed foolish to both them and to me. What did *thirst* have to do with *drinking*? It became a point of honor on both sides.

"Drink, you bastard!" they were silently shouting at me and I replied as silently, "Not on your life, you dead shits."

I refused again and again until the fury in the offering person's eyes was matched only by the look in my own. I have never felt so much fury.

A whole conglomeration of other feelings and thoughts also raged in my mind: the trouble alcohol had brought the place. I had seen children in the street after lunch not returning to school because the Shell refused to serve them. The children were hungry from lack of breakfast. Their parents were still sleeping after a big night being charged. Lunch was their first, perhaps their only, meal and the Shell people insisted on serving them last after every other customer no matter what order they had arrived in the shop, meaning they would be late returning to school where they would be held in after school as a result. This was a punishment worse than death. It was better, therefore, not to go back to school at all for the afternoon.

Watching the swaying, slurring people was bringing alternate waves of despair and revolt to my heart. I had decided I ought not to be hung over for the next day's activities based on some puritanical notion that I needed to be my best for the next day's work.

And I didn't like the pressure this person was exerting on me to drink. I hate that. I hate being told to do things. Being treated like a petulant child by some teacher figure getting off on the power they are wielding over me. I have never been so close to punching someone out. I would have, could have, if things around me weren't quite so distracting and the fact punching a lawyer mightn't be such a good way to start in this town.

I stood sullenly next to Victor, who was also looking somewhat bewildered. Katy and Keith were doing their own things elsewhere. Arms folded, it was clear I was not having fun and had no intention of having any. I should have left and gone back to the motel and been miserable by myself.

But in hindsight maybe I knew there was still something else to happen. That this place—a place I find provocative every time I go there, where I still get lost each time I visit there—there still could be, would be, something else.

Two people moved forwards to talk, or so I assumed, with Victor. I was standing on the edge of the interaction as I often do. This life doesn't include me, I seem to be stating, but really I am wanting not to intrude in something that everyone else is a part of, but somehow I do not include me in "everyone." Nervously I was listening in to the conversation, trying to look bored. Trying to look both included and excluded simultaneously in a method I have developed to protect me both ways.

Victor began to talk with them of some issues in town he knows a little about. They explained they have been fighting for years to gain ownership of land some distance out of town which is theirs and is crucial to their wellbeing. They mentioned they can take us there if we have time for a visit. This land is extraordinary and we must go, they explained. It looked as though finally things were moving and it could be back in their hands any moment. We have to go and see it. They swayed in front of us, telling us about their struggle to have their connection to it recognized, holding their bottles of beer by their long necks, pointing them at us, jabbing them in our direction as they spoke. There was a long silence then as they regained their balance, and before anything more was said,

"Where are you from?" they asked.

Victor started to answer. He had explained to me a few times already about his family. They had had an extremely tough time and he has done well for himself. He was the first one from the family who has got through the whole of the school system and attended university. He worked hard for everything he has achieved. He was proud of where he had got but was still awkward with himself, I could tell. He looked awkwardly around seeking help in this conversation.

But they stopped him mid-answer and asked again, waving their arms and hands, pointing vaguely at us with the beers they are holding.

"Who are you? Where are you from?" they asked again.

Victor understood the protocols, as he was an Aboriginal person himself although not from that particular place. He went to answer and to talk of his family and his Country, which wasn't far away as the crow flies. But he was stopped once again.

This time, the two stilled their waving arms temporarily. Both nodded directly at me and waved their partly filled bottles straight at me.

"No, this one 'ere. You. We know you." they said, stabbing the long necks towards me. "Watsya-name?"

We were in a crowded room with blanked out windows and closed doors. There was a raucous drunken rabble crammed all around, an incredible noise of everyone talking all at once. And at that moment, I was transported to outside. Into an immense landscape's silence.

They leaned in, these two, with their beers, to listen more closely to what I was about to say, as I looked curiously at the shoes on my feet which seemed to be moving at a fast rate into the vast distance.

They elbowed Victor aside, nudged into my personal space and focused their attention on me. They wanted to hear what they didn't really need to hear me say.

Before I even have a chance to speak, they nodded together.

"Yeah, of course, ya Roddy's niece. We know you. You're from here. You're one of us!"

They beamed.

"You're from here. You're one of us!" The words seemed to wake me up to a thing that had needed attention.

Who was I? Where did I belong? What did belonging mean? Where did I come from? What did it mean to know where you came from? How did you, how would you, know where you came from, apart from what you had been told—and what if you had not been told much at all? Don't we all want to know this at various times of our life?

Could it be that I belonged here?

"Where are you from?"

It sounds an ordinary question, something anyone might ask at some time or other. But here in this country—

in Aboriginal Countries—it means something more. It establishes your place and your connection to everywhere else.

Families divide quickly into his and her side. Which do you follow? Which do you own? Which owns you? Which part do you belong to? Which part do you long-to-be with? Where do you want to be placed? Who defines who and how?

I defined myself through my mother's family and their beliefs. More particularly I defined myself through my mother's father's family. On my mother's father's side, there seemed to be a clear straight line going back decades. But in fact even her family was not simple.

What of my mother's mother's family of my grandmother's claims to being Aboriginal? Of my cousins telling me their mother, my aunty, was called a black gin? Of my mother's father saying his wife was from "the wrong side of the tracks?"

What of my father's side? It was rarely spoken of.

I had always thought of myself as being my mother's daughter.

Now suddenly I was being claimed as a part of my father's family.

It was not what I had expected. I knew very little about my father's family—only that my grandfather had died when I was very young and that my grandparents were cousins. I knew that my father had connections to "out west" close to where I was now hanging around in a pub but not much more detail than that. Here were people saying they knew me, although I had never been there before, never met them.

Was this a part I had been missing all along? I didn't know who Roddy was. I didn't remember his name from our list of workshop participants for the next day. Yet somehow these people were identifying me as associated with him—even before they knew my name or knew who I was.

There are few leads to my father's family. He had no brothers or sisters. Both his parents died while I was still at school.

Could I be related to Roddy? Absolutely but how would I know?

CONGRUENCE

I RETURNED TO MY WORK squatting in red dirt on the edge of a town on the edge of a concrete block house on the edge of a concrete dunny path, on the edge of my heels, on edge with a group of people.

Talking with people who live on the edge of town is one part of my work I love.

This is the hard edge of life. There is little softness here. No feathering only a hard line between this and that. The placement of everything isn't quite so precious. It tends to shock and I enjoy the possibilities associated with this. Maybe it isn't a question of liking at all but one of acceptance. The instant coffee I have been given with its almost off milk is luke-warm, but the spirit of generosity with which it has been offered makes up for it. I am sketching squiggles in the dirt with a stick. We don't say much.

It is impossible to predict what will happen out here. Sometimes everything goes well and I manage to get through all the tasks I want to complete. Sometimes nothing at all gets done. People mightn't be at home. People might have changed houses or locations even. People are still asleep and seem impossible to wake. People are drunk and disorderly and spill out from their house shouting and screaming at…could be you, could be someone else, could be nothing in particular. People can be incredibly generous and share their last drops of cordial with you. A task that should take a few hours can take days. On most days, I am awash with tea and coffee and cordial. Sometimes though things can be tricky. You need to be able to tell at an instant how things are likely to proceed and whether to abandon your mission and move onto something else.

I struggle though the salt-bush and knock tentatively on a caravan's door. People jump out from a concrete block-house adjoining the caravan and mumble the caravan dwellers aren't home. When I ask, I am advised those I am after either don't live there anymore or they are out of town. I can't quite understand what is explained to me. Maybe who I am after never did live there. The advisors disappear back into their concrete block-house and the door is slammed shut.

The heat is pounding.

In the background, I notice there is someone collecting sticks and branches. Every now and then she hisses at me. I stand, clip board and pencil case tidily held, camera too, uncertain if she is indicating I should go over or stay away. I try to look certain, confident, organized. My hair gives me away. No matter how many times I brush or comb it, it remains airy and flies around messily.

She waddles over to me finally. She has bowed legs just like my grandmother, a toothless grin and ever watchful, mischievous eyes. She motions for me to come and sit a while with her. I follow her back to her place where she sits down on a broken chair near a circle of stones. I have an edge of concrete path to squat on. She leans forward slowly, legs wide apart and throws a match onto the sticks she has collected. On one side of the chair a billy (a wire-handled metal can used for cooking on an open fire) is hanging, filled with water. After we have been sitting for a considerable time, and when the fire is just right, she balances the billy on the fire.

"Tea?" she asks.

I nod and we sit watching the water come to the boil. She throws in the tea-leaves. When the tea is ready, she pours it from the billy into some chipped enameled cups. There is no milk but plenty of sugar. We sit silently sipping the strong sweet tea. Finally, she waves at me and says:

"Your name, your name."

"Where are you from? Who are you?" she asks.

As I explain to her the bits I know such as my mother's missionary family, I tell her about being called out in her town. What does it mean? Before I have finished she is nodding. "Hmmm. Mmmm."

She is nodding. "Hmmm."

She goes on to say I should simply say to anyone who asks what I have just told her.

"They will understand!" she says.

No more is said. I instantly want to know about her life. She has no further interest in mine. She knows all she needs to know.

There were so many Aboriginal people who were taken from their family to be raised as white—or taken from their family to be used as servants in a white family—or who were too afraid to ever say who they really were. It was better to say you were a gypsy, than to admit to being Aboriginal. There was talk at one point that Aboriginal people would disappear, that they were a dying race and the colonizers did their best to make this happen.

It never did. Aboriginal people continue to fight for their rights, to fight to be seen as the original inhabitants here. The land was never ceded. Always was, always will be Aboriginal land.

Next time I see her, I want recognition. But it could never be. She is sitting in town under the broad veranda tacked to the side of the pub. There is a single seat there although more seats under the shade could have been provided. Her gaze is through me now—much the same as many of the others standing and leaning against the wall. She focuses nowhere. It is pension day after all. I hover uncertainly but don't go forward. I want to. I want to remind her of our cup of tea together but am afraid to start the conversation. I swap my clipboard and pencil case nervously into the other hand and walk on to the motel.

HOLDING THE THREADS

HOMEBODY

Home | hone | bone | bode | body
Home | tome | time | tile | till | tell | sell | self

Home. Body. Self. All the same. All paths lead there
and back. Sometimes it takes longer to return than it did
setting out.
   I am still "me": I am still "home"—wherever it is.
   The path was perhaps shorter than I had imagined.
I wanted everyone to be there—my mother, my father,
my grandparents and theirs.
   I wanted everything to be there—home, body, aikido,
place.
   But Chomei never tried to accommodate everything.
He spoke only of himself. He saw himself as a single
silkworm. I too see this but my threads are interwoven
with so many others.
   As I write I keep losing the thread.

Just as in life as I keep losing favorite books.
   I want to check something in *Pilgrim at Tinker
Creek*—I can't find it.
   There is something else to look at in *The Cows*—I
can't find it.
   I think of *Reading the Country*—I can't find it.

I can find none of the books I want to refer to. When I can't find a copy after searching and searching, I order another copy. Usually when I do this, the original book turns up the day after the new copy arrives.

When I read the book I thought I needed, I find nothing of what I wanted.

(Trust me to become bogged down in something unimportant.)

The truth is I want to find a book which will show me how to end, how to find me. I can think of none.

After days and days of writing and searching, I realize that everything is right there before me—hiding behind those other books where I didn't look.

I wanted my homecoming to be joyous. I wanted to be recognized. I wanted to recognize myself as I arrived. It wasn't to be.

I should know this. A house is merely an external shell that needs to be reshaped to suit.

All I needed to do was to spend more time—more time with myself, meeting me.

I wanted certainty and have been driven to find it. But I am becoming more certain of my uncertainty and maybe this is fine too. I am none of these things and all of them.

I never do trace my family back to identify them all. My father was an only child—or that is how I know him. Roddy? Roddy could be a relative but I never get any closer to him than hearing his name. There are Aboriginal Barlows—my father's mother and father were cousins but I know no more than that.

I can keep searching of course but in the end what else do I need to know. What else would convince me? If the very land sings to me, what else might I expect?

I don't believe in the binary one or other.

I don't believe in Male/Female; Us/Them—we are all continuums even if this does make things more difficult and less tidy.

Architects no longer assume that everything must be straight and in-line. Gaudi's Sagrada Familia Cathedral is decomposing as the very same time as it is being composed and built. It is a marvel none-the-less!

I struggle with the idea in aikido that *nage/uke*—fighter/defender are one and the same—yet it is a key principle. Every now and then I understand or intuit this and then it is gone again. Grasping hold of it immediately separates it and hence destroys it.

WHERE DO YOU COME FROM?

I DO UNDERSTAND, of course, that I am meant to tidy this up now and present the reader with a package so they feel fulfilled. I did warn at the beginning that this would not be one of those texts that resolves itself. I started out secretly hoping that this is what would happen. It hasn't. Just as life for most Aboriginal people never resolves itself to be easier and to run smoothly for them. Everything has to change.

For Aboriginal people to thrive, we all need to be culturally safe—which involves self-reflection and truth telling about the history in Australia. Our telling of these truths, our listening to them, without necessarily joining them neatly together, being responsible for our own part creates the map to Country.

In the end, I know where Country sings to me, I know those people who welcome me "home." I know where I want to belong but things don't always sit comfortably like that. Life is complicated—more so if you make it.

In the end, I don't entirely agree with Chomei in the Hojoki. We don't need things, or answers but we do need to care about each other absolutely and then we will know about the world and ourselves and "be at home."

If one knows himself and knows what the world is, he will merely wish for quiet and be pleased when he has nothing to grieve about, wanting nothing and caring for nobody. (The Hojoki, 18)

BIBLIOGRAPHY

Alexander, C., Silverstein, Ishikawa, Silverstein, Jacobson, Fiksdahl-King, & Angel. (1982). A pattern language: Towns buildings construction. Oxford University Press.

Benterrak, K., Muecke, S., & Roe, P. (1984). Reading the country: Fremantle Arts Centre Press.

Brooks, B. (2009). The verandah notebooks. Outskirts: Feminism along the Edge, 20 (May).

Carter, P., & Lewis, R. (1999). Depth of translation: The book of raft. NMA Publications.

Chomei. (1979). The ten foot square hut and tales of the Heike: Being two thirteenth-century Japanese classics, the "Hojoki" and selections from the "Heike Monogatari." (A. L. Sadler, Trans.; Fifth). Charles E. Tuttle Company.

Chomei, K. no. (2011). Natsume Soseki's English translation of Hojoki (W. Ridgeway, Ed.; N. Soseki, Trans.). Kindle ebook.

Davis, L. (2011). The Cows. Sarabande Books.

Delueze, G., & Guattari, F. (1994). A thousand plateaus: Capitalism and schizophrenia. University of Minnesota Press.

Dillard, A. (2007). Pilgrim at Tinker Creek. Harper Perennial.

Gibbs, A. (1997). Bodies and words: Feminism and fictocriticism—Explanation and demonstration. TEXT Journal, 1(2).

Gibbs, A. (2005). Fictocriticism, Affect, mimesis: Engendering differences. TEXT Journal, 9(1).

Goodall, H. (1996). Invasion to embassy: Land in Aboriginal politics in New South Wales. Allen & Unwin.

Kerr, H., & Nettelbeck, A. (Eds.). (1998). The space between: Australian women writing fictocriticism. University of Western Australia Press.

Kincaid, J. (1999). My garden (book). Farrar, Strauss and Giroux.

Le Corbusier. (1967). The modulor (P. De Francia & A. Bostock, Trans.). Faber & Faber.

Le Corbusier. (1974). Towards a new architecture. The Architectural Press.

Le Corbusier. (1981). Une petite maison. Architektur Artemis.

Le Plastrier, R. (2011). Ma.

Memmott, P. (1991). Humpy, house and tin shed: Aboriginal settlement history on the Darling river. Ian Buchan Fell Research Centre.

Neale, M. (2017). Songlines: Tracking the seven sisters. National Museum of Australia.

Nitschke, G. (1966). "Ma" the Japanese sense of "place" in old and new architecture and planning. Architectural Design, 34, 116-156.

Prosser, R. (2009). Fragments of a Fictocritical Dictionary. Outskirts: Feminism along the Edge, 20(May).

Schumacher, E. F. (1993). Small is Beautiful.

Sen, N. (2017). The Songkeepers.

Shonagon, S. (2006). The pillow book (M. Mckinney, Trans.). Penguin Classics.

Strehlow, T. G. H. (2015). Journey to Horseshoe Bend. Giramondo Press.

ACKNOWLEDGEMENTS

I am grateful to many, many people who have pushed me along the way to completing this book. First up it must be Saddle Road Press, Ruth Thompson and Don Mitchell, who so generously put me up in their home and have given me this incredible opportunity to have my book published. They also have taught me much about the whole process thank you Ruth and Don, you don't know what you have given me.

Then there is my family—Daniel and Max have lived through the long hours I have spent writing and worrying about it—and my mum!

I also want to acknowledge Michel Wing and Nola Farman for their editing work and still, any mistakes are mine.

I want to thank Dr. Anna Gibbs who believed in my writing enough to get me to start (and complete) a PhD.

To Dr. Juanita Sherwood who has been one of the best friends ever and whose wise advice and assistance has always been given very generously.

Have I mentioned the many women I met through A Room Of Her Own Foundation (AROHO)? including Dr. Carrie Nassif, Tanya Pryputniewicz and Bhanu Kapil.

I want to acknowledge the Gadigal people of the Eora Nation on whose land I wrote this book and have lived for decades now.

Always was, always will be Aboriginal land.

ABOUT THE AUTHOR

Gillian Barlow is a writer and registered architect. She has had stories published in a variety of journals. She has a PhD from the Writing and Society Group, University of Western Sydney. Her exegesis was on Aboriginal housing from which this book emerged. For most of her career, she has worked in housing and health, particularly Aboriginal housing and primary health buildings as well as in disability housing. She has  written guidelines as to how to do these. She was awarded a Gold Premier's Award for her work with Communities on an Employment and Training Program.

She was selected and attended twice the residencies with A Room Of Her Own (AROHO) in New Mexico, USA. In 2019, she was a writing fellow at Can Serrat, Catalonia and will again stay at Can Serrat in October, 2022.

She lives in Sydney, Australia, with her partner where she works as a researcher on cultural safety and a range of First Nations' projects.

She continues to train in aikido.

Her website is gillianhbarlow.com.au

Lightning Source UK Ltd.
Milton Keynes UK
UKHW011117160223
417122UK00006B/737